AF394728

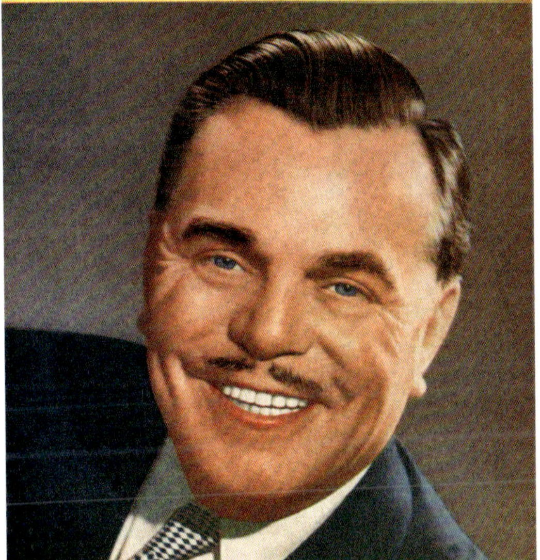

HULLO CAMPERS!

UNTIL we meet again in the sunshine, here's a friendly word from myself and all the members of the Redcoat staff to let you know we're thinking of you. Roll on summer and the happy days that lie ahead !

Sincerely

Billy Butlin

In the series *Vintage Britain*

BOOK ONE
The East End in Colour
1960–1980

BOOK TWO
The Isle of Dogs

BOOK THREE
Dog Show
1961–1978

BOOK FOUR
Paradise Street

BOOK FIVE
The East End in Colour
1980–1990

BOOK SIX
London Underground
1970–1980

BOOK SEVEN
Hackney Archive

BOOK EIGHT
Butlin's Holiday Camp 1982

BUTLIN'S HOLIDAY CAMP 1982

BARRY LEWIS

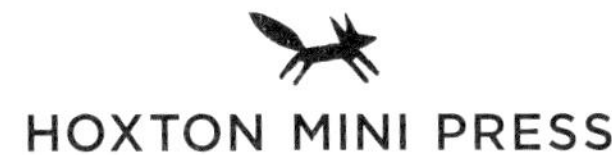

HOXTON MINI PRESS

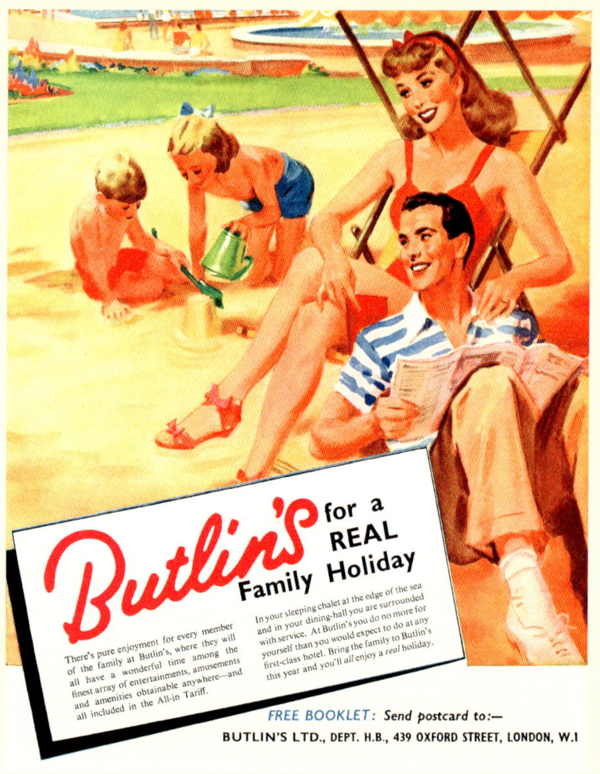

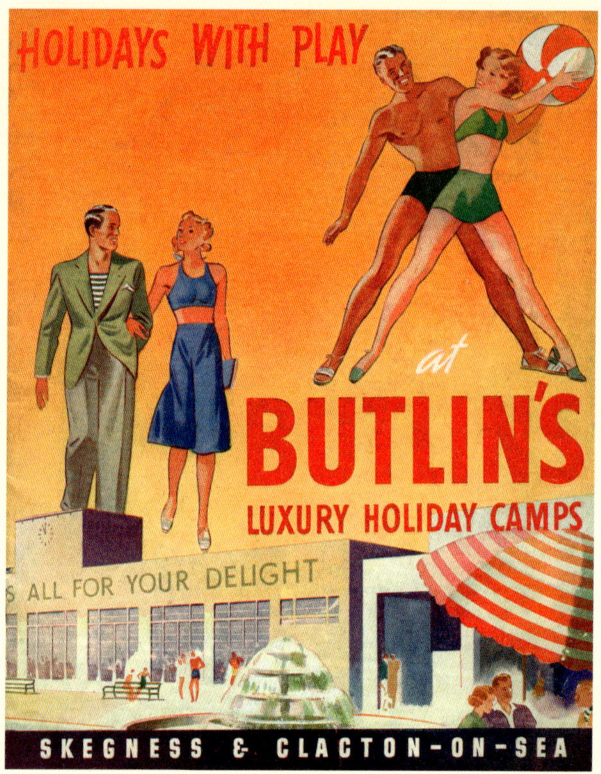

Above left: Butlin's magazine advertisement, c.1953
Above right: Front cover of Butlin's sales brochure, 1939

INTRODUCTION

In 1936, Billy Butlin had a dream that changed the face of British holidays.

Born into a fairground family, he was a natural entrepreneur who started his career on the Skegness seafront, running sideshows such as the infamous 'Daredevil Peggy, a one-legged diver who plunged 60 foot into a shallow tank of blazing water!' He even brought the first bumper cars – 'dodgems' – to Britain. After bad experiences in seaside B&Bs, when he was locked out of his room all day by unrepentant landladies, he dreamt up a vision of providing affordable 'all-in' holidays for ordinary British families. In 1934 he bought 200 acres of a former turnip field close to the beach near Skegness for £3,000 and set about creating a self-contained 'holiday village' for families and young children.

'My plans were for 1,000 people in 600 chalets with electricity, running water, 250 bathrooms, dining and recreational halls. There would be a theatre, a gymnasium, a rhododendron-bordered swimming pool with cascades at both ends and a boating lake.'

Butlin's idea was to create a miniature seaside resort, an enclosed fantasy world, for its residents to echo the lives of the rich and famous as seen in the popular movies and magazines. The look was 1930s deco style with vast dining rooms, bars and ballrooms, with grand features designed to create an atmosphere of luxury for working people. The intriguing invitation to the camp, emblazoned across a building overlooking the swimming pool, was the phrase: 'Our true intent is all for your delight', a quote from Shakespeare's *A Midsummer Night's Dream,* which Butlin spotted on the side of a fairground organ.

This glamorous vision was only a veneer as everything had to be done on the cheap. Butlin's slogan, 'A week's holiday for a week's pay', coincided with The Holiday Pay Act 1938, when many working-class Britons got their first taste of sun, sea and sand. Here was a self-contained holiday experience that provided you with three meals a day and a wealth of entertainment for £1.75 a week.

Always about showmanship, the official grand opening was performed by Amy Johnson, the first woman to fly solo from London to Australia, and the concept proved so popular that by the time Butlin's opened on a cold, snowy Easter in 1936, it was already fully booked for the whole summer season.

Entertainment in the camps was initially home-grown, with the newly formed Redcoats (entertainment staff who were often aspiring performers) brightening a rainy day by telling a few jokes to the campers after supper in the dining halls. Eventually each camp had radio and theatre stars visiting weekly while their own resident orchestras played the dance hits of the era. There was always a tradition of singalongs, led by the Redcoats, in the bars and dance halls – with unique Butlin's lyrics set to familiar tunes. Although these songs were fading away by the 1980s, some verses have been included throughout this book as they epitomise the spirit of the camps.

Dance competitions were held throughout the summer and the Butlin's competition became the biggest in the world – the *Strictly Come Dancing* of its day. In 1962 Paul McCartney and John Lennon came to the Skegness camp to ask Ringo Starr, who was drumming for the resident band, if he'd be interested in joining The Beatles. The rest is history.

Competitions were big in general: the famous Knobbly Knees contest was once judged by comedy legends Laurel and Hardy, and the idea for the Glamorous Grandmother contest came when Billy met the actress Marlene Dietrich in America and was stunned to find she was a grandmother.

At the beginning of the Second World War the Skegness camp was taken over by the Royal Navy for military training and re-named H.M.S Royal Arthur. Several times it was hit by Nazi bombs and even at one point declared sunk! After the end of the war, canny Billy organised a deal with the government and in 1946, within just six weeks, it had re-opened for campers.

Over 30 years, a total of nine UK camps were built. These can be divided into three distinct eras: the pre-war camps of Skegness (1936) and Clacton (1938); the wartime camps of Filey (1939), Pwllheli (1940) and Ayr (1940), and the post-war camps of

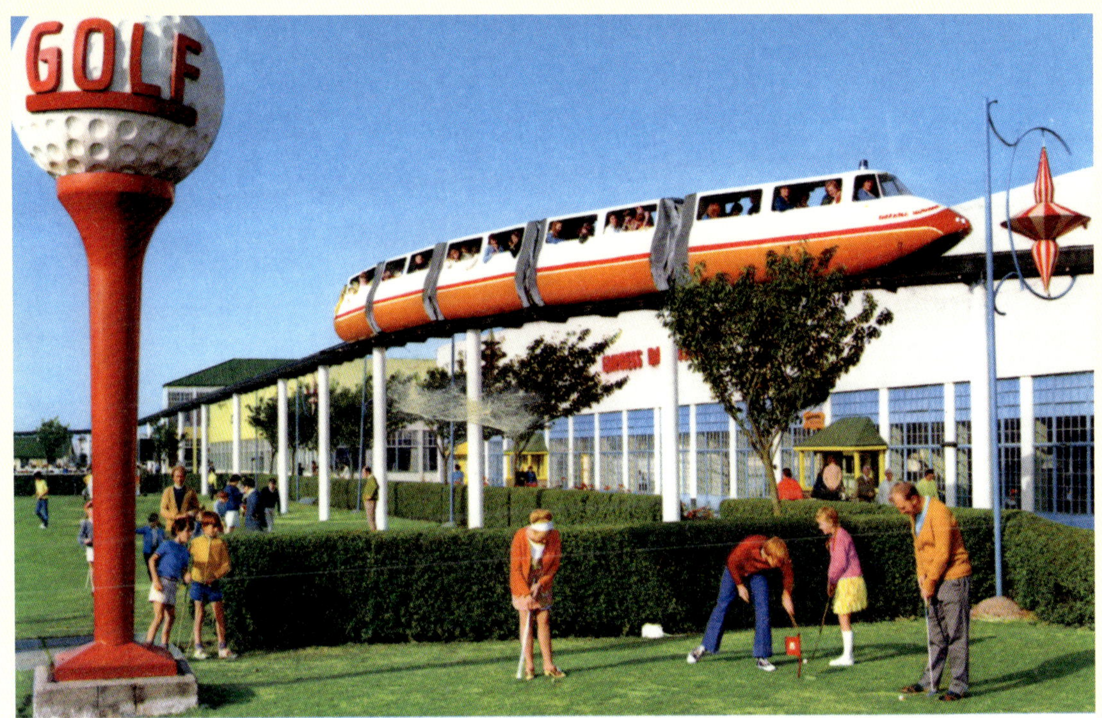

Butlin's Skegness postcard, c.1971

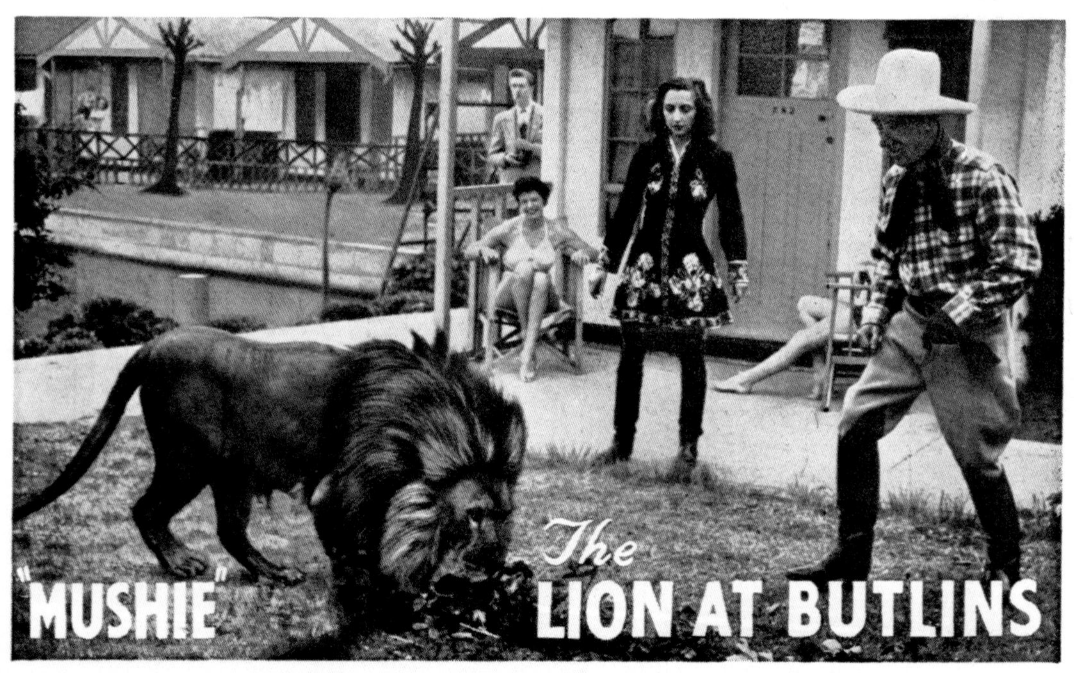

Butlin's Clacton postcard, 1955

Mosney (1948), Bognor (1960), Minehead (1962) and Barry (1966). Each camp was developed into a mini town and was virtually self-sufficient. Most were equipped with shopping arcades, indoor and outdoor pools, sporting and entertainment facilities, fairgrounds, bars and discos, theatres, amusements, boating lakes, churches, hairdressing salons, newsagents, betting shops, launderettes, post offices, chairlifts, miniature railways and by 1965, the Skegness and Minehead camps even had a monorail!

Billy Butlin had always loved both animals and the publicity they produced. He used to drive around town with a lion cub in the back of his car, and elephants and lions were often seen in the camps. One famous visitor was Mushie the lion, safe around the campers because he had no teeth. The zoos in the camps finished in the 1950s but elephants were kept on for rides and parades until Gertie, a 28-year-old Indian elephant, drowned in the Skegness swimming pool in 1962. Getting him out proved a nightmare: a Redcoat lifeguard had to dive into the murky brown water to attach chains to the animal and the crane crashed with the weight.

Steve, Gertie's minder, sobbed continually (but later claimed her foot as an umbrella stand!)

My own Butlin's experience started in the summer of 1966 when I worked as a kitchen porter in one of the huge kitchens in the Bognor camp. It was my first job after school and I learned all about work, love and booze! I developed an odd affection for this enclosed, parallel universe that was fun, different and full of possibilities. It was my first emancipation from the claustrophobia of home and school in the London suburbs, both scary and exciting. This feeling of escapism was captured in the words of Frank Barnes, an assistant catering manager at Skegness: 'The news doesn't count here... when you go off-camp at the end of the season, it doesn't matter that you didn't know the road tax had gone up again... the camp is a cloud-cuckoo land. If you can't face reality, it's a great place.'

Returning 16 years later, in the early 1980s, to photograph the Skegness camp for the *Observer Magazine*, was like returning to a dream that had become a little darker. By now Butlin's was at a low ebb as Brits were being enticed abroad by cheap foreign package deals and holiday camps by the 'bracing' British seaside were losing their appeal. There was also a decrease in the number of families booking holidays and in their place came groups of young singles with money in their pockets, ready for a wilder time.

By the time Billy Butlin died in 1981, there was a problem with decaying camp conditions and the rather tarnished Butlin's 'Hi De Hi!' image that harked back to an earlier era. In 1987 the family business was sold, most chalets were demolished, new 'superpools' built and the entire business rebranded.

Now, in 2020, Butlin's appears to be booming again, benefitting from the trends and anxieties of Brexit-era Britain – including a weak currency that has made foreign destinations more expensive; fears about terrorism and security, and a hard-to-quantify yearning for British style nostalgia.

My photographs from over 35 years ago seem to be looking even further back, to a vanished age – the hair and clothing styles, the attitudes, the activities, the wartime buildings – with a certain innocence, in a world before mobile phones and the internet, where a holiday was annual and special, making everyone determined to enjoy themselves to the full, whatever the weather!

Barry Lewis
London, 2020

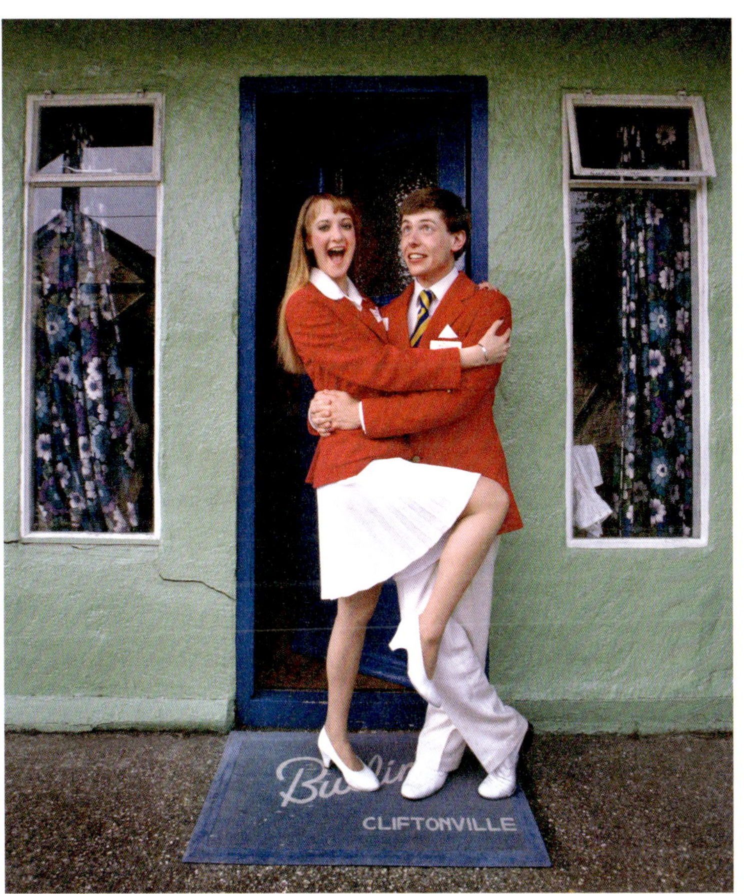

Butlins
CLIFTONVILLE

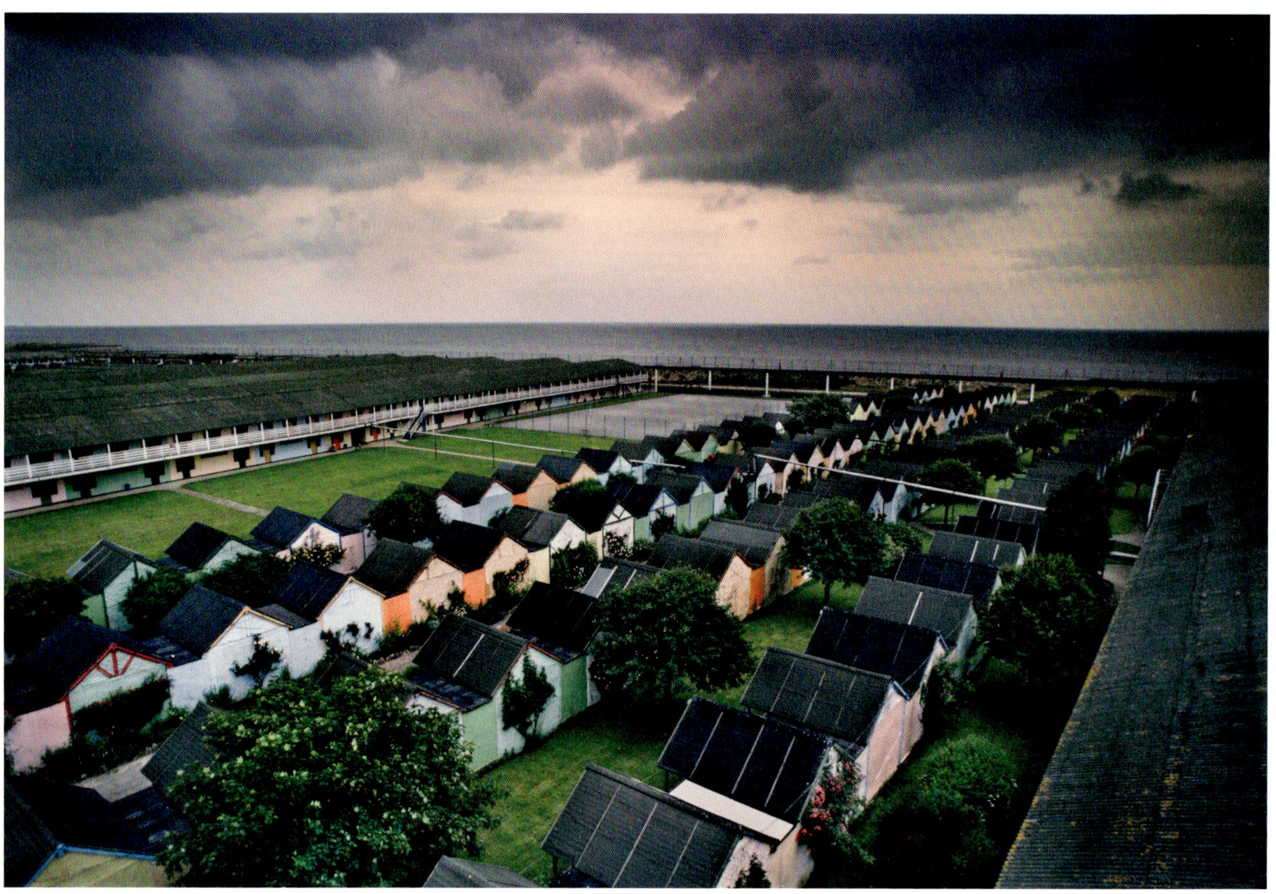

The new form of holiday camp gives you this
essential privacy in the shape of a hut or
chalet made of concrete, timber and asbestos
sheet roofing... But added to this privacy,
and not conflicting with it, the new sort of camping
provides as much social life and as much play
and pleasure as you can desire and can endure.

Tom Wintringham, 'Picture Post', 1939

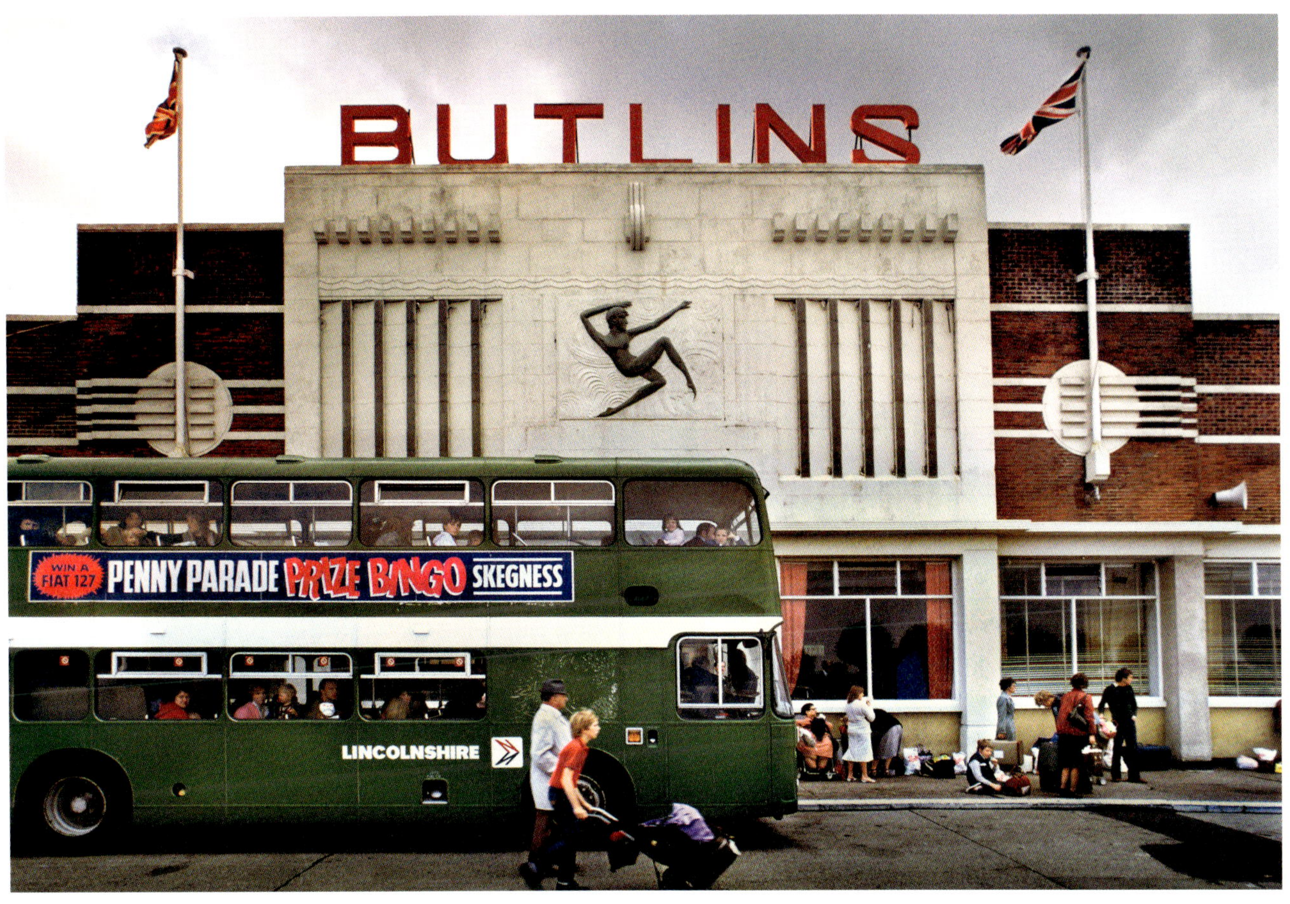

A busy week at Butlin's began each Saturday morning with thousands of new campers arriving by car, bus and train.

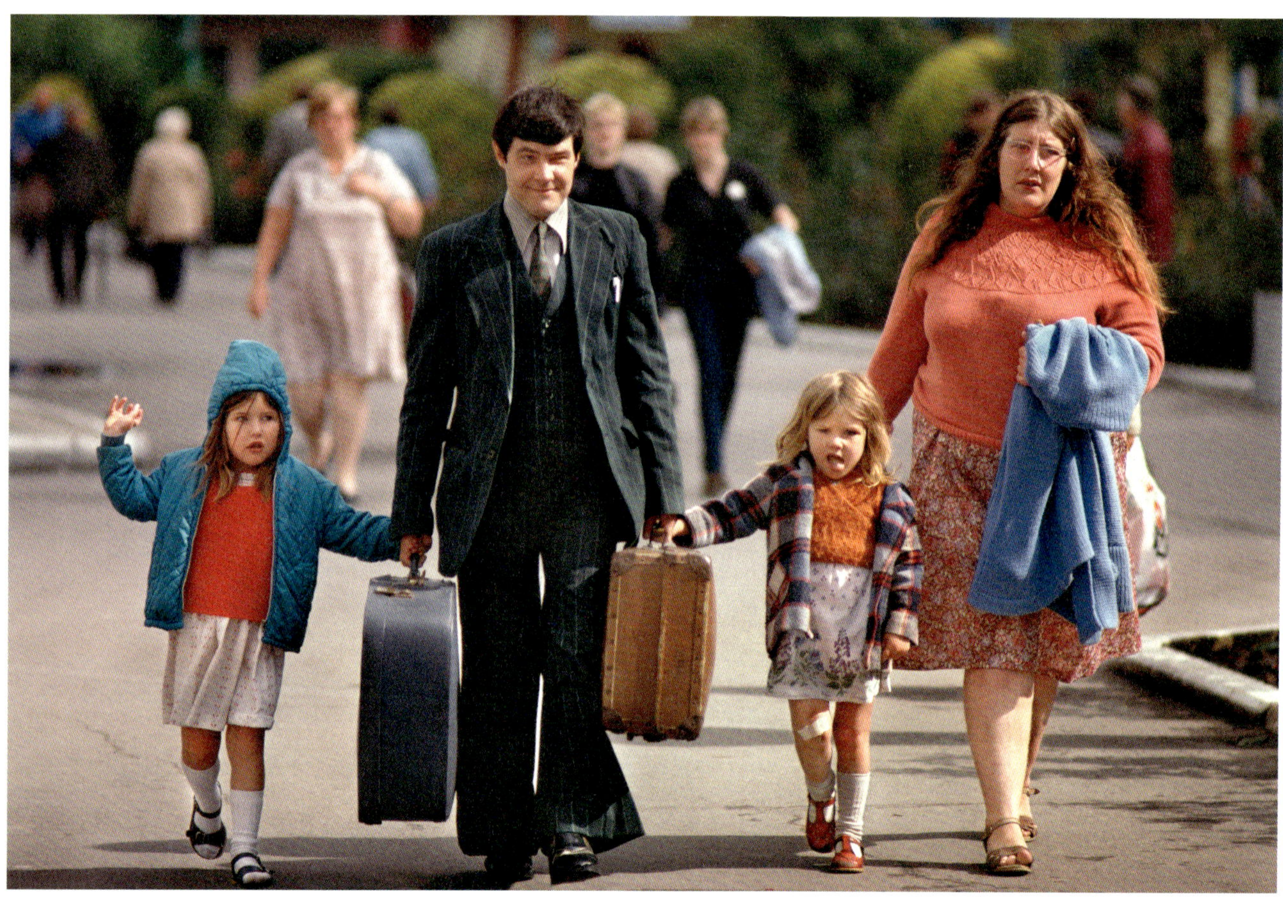

We all came down to Butlin's, Butlin's by the sea
Now we're all as happy, as happy as can be
Tramp, Tramp, Tramp, Tramp, hear the call
Hi-De-Hi, Ho-De-Ho!

Extract from the song 'Tramp Tramp Tramp', derived from
an American Civil War song 'The Prisoner's Hope'

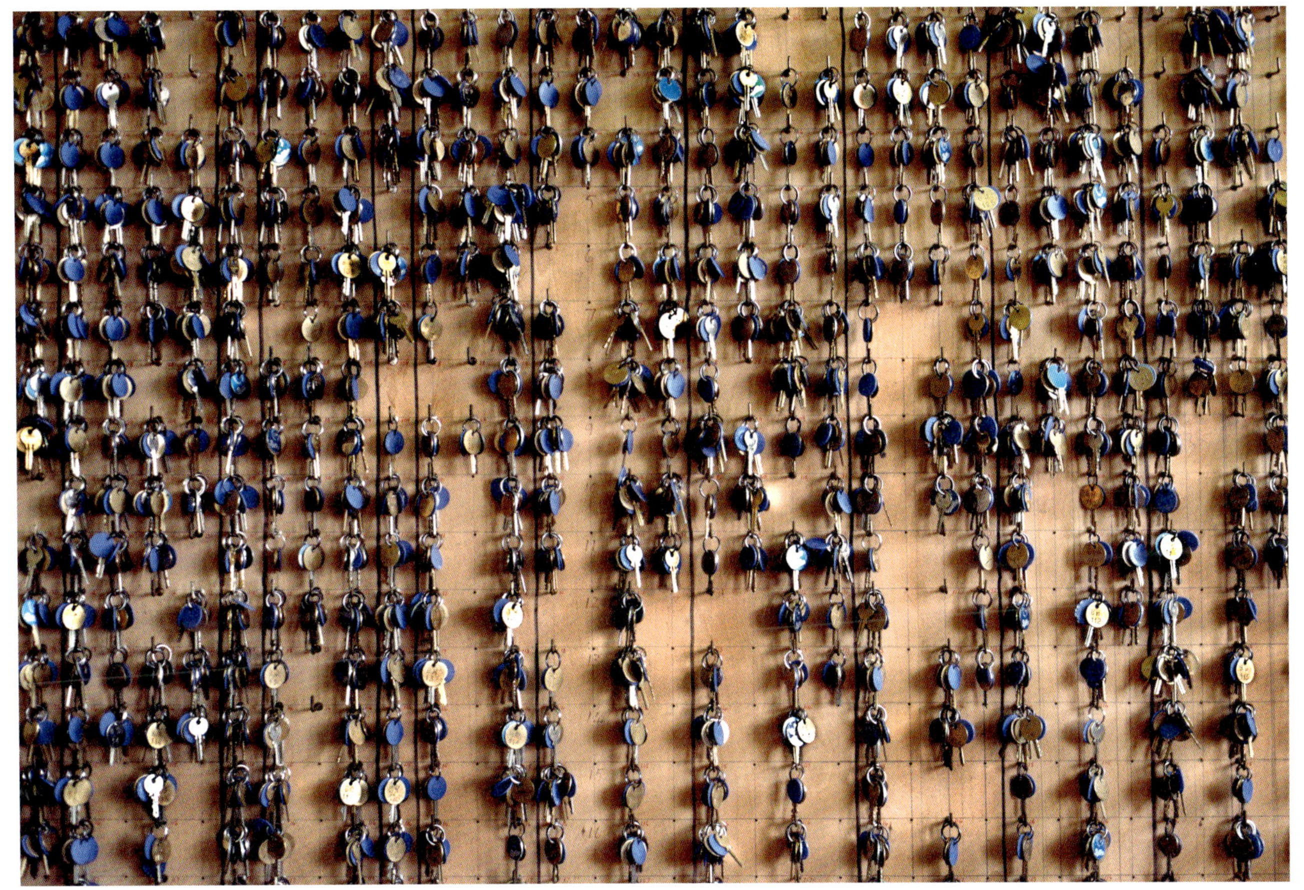

Keys to the chalets at camp reception.

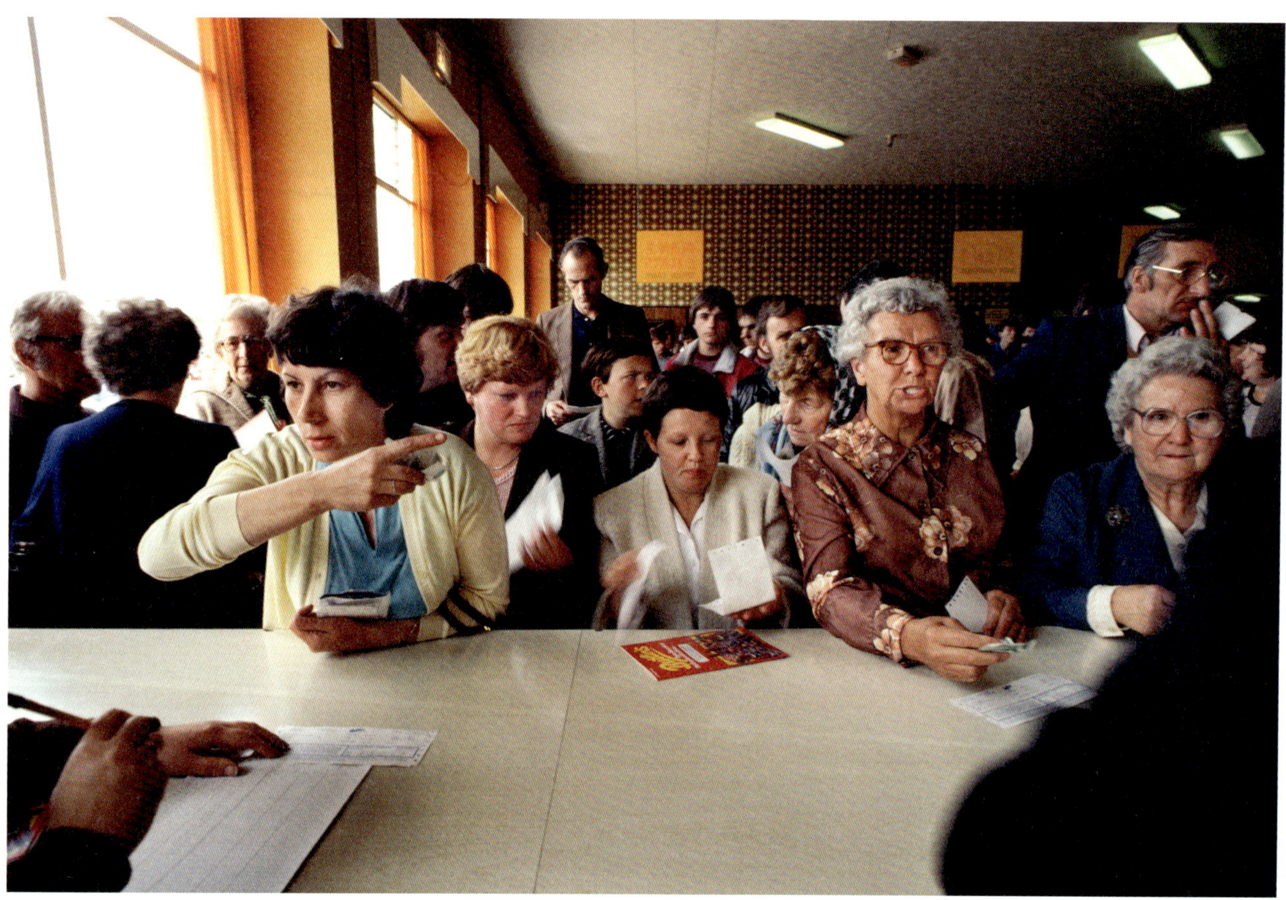

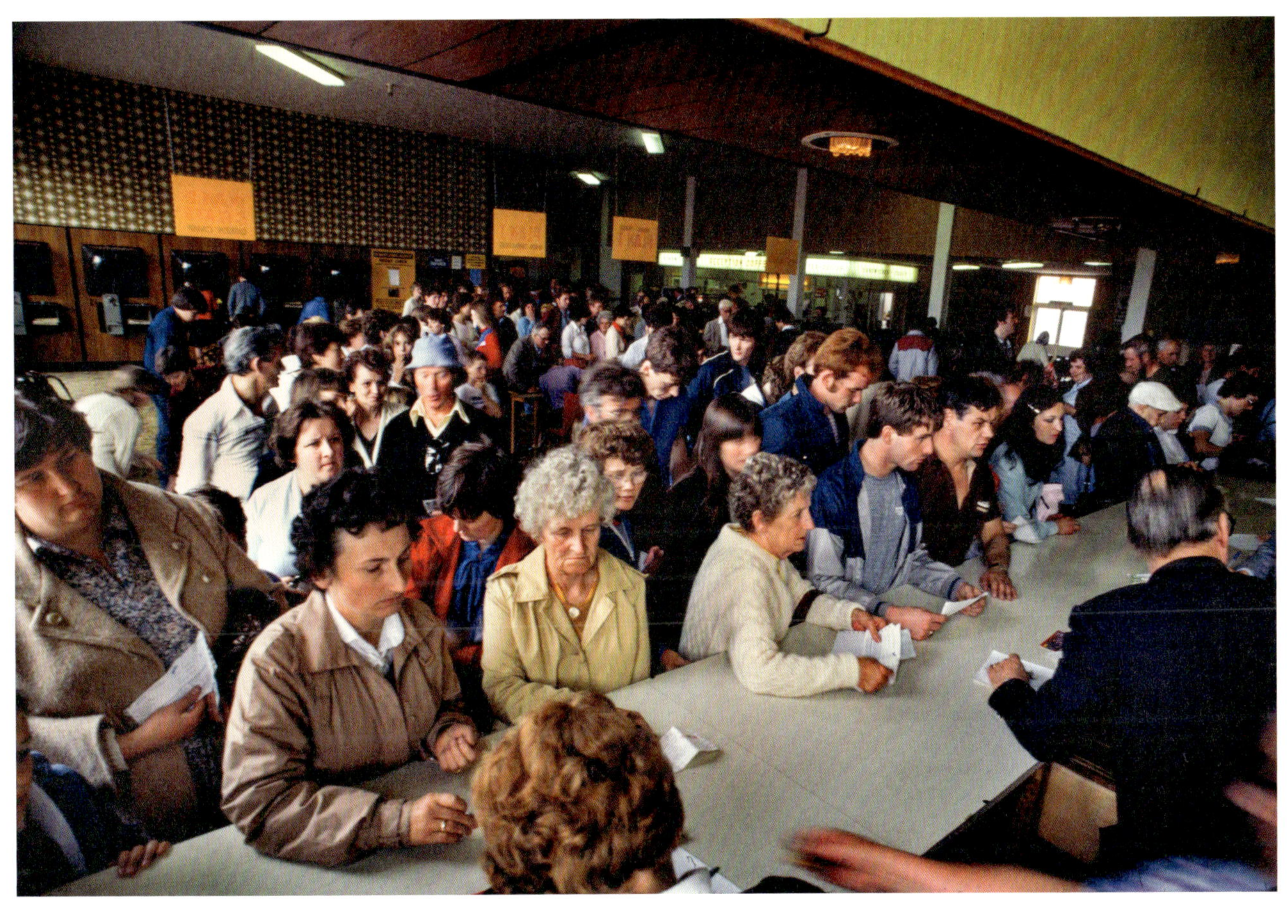

New arrivals checking in.

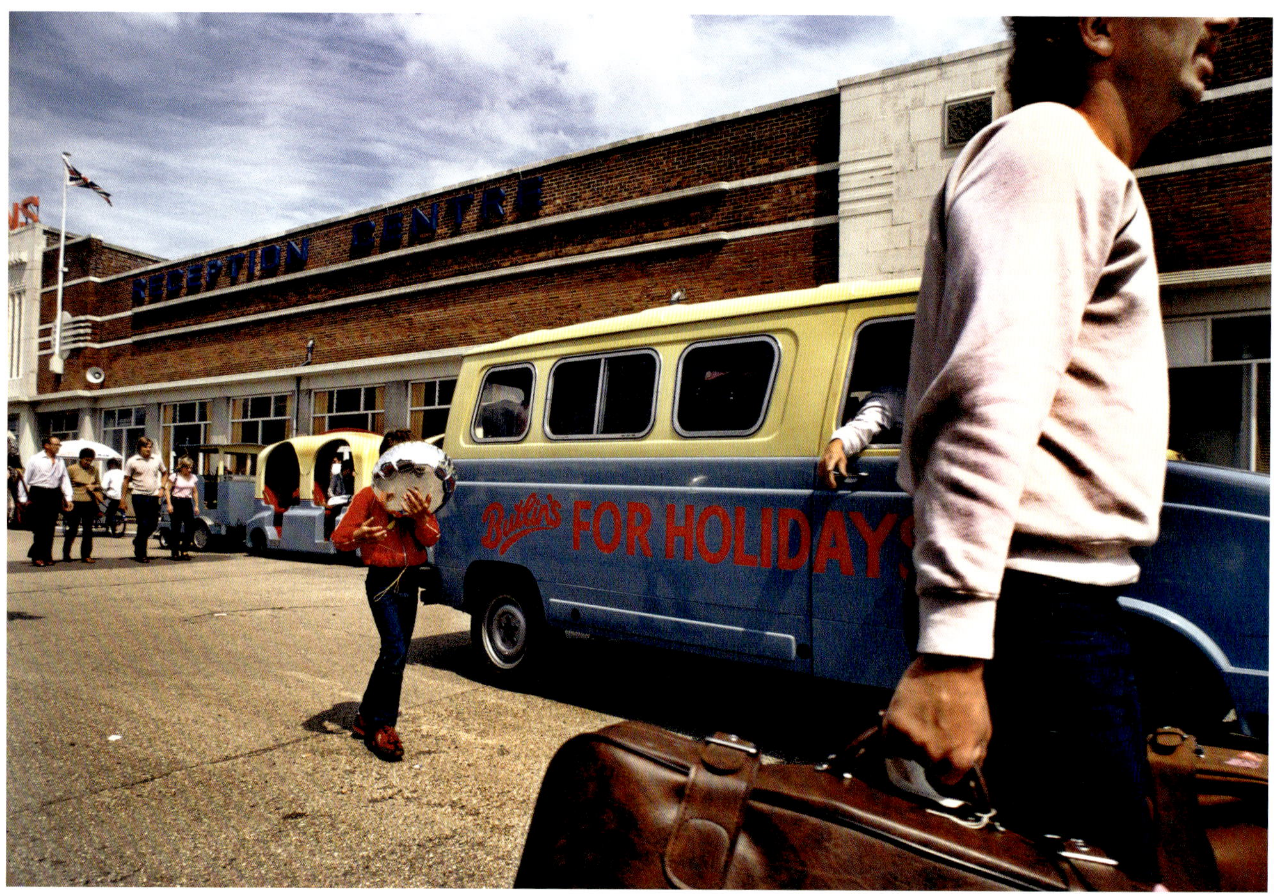
RECEPTION CENTRE
Butlin's FOR HOLIDAYS

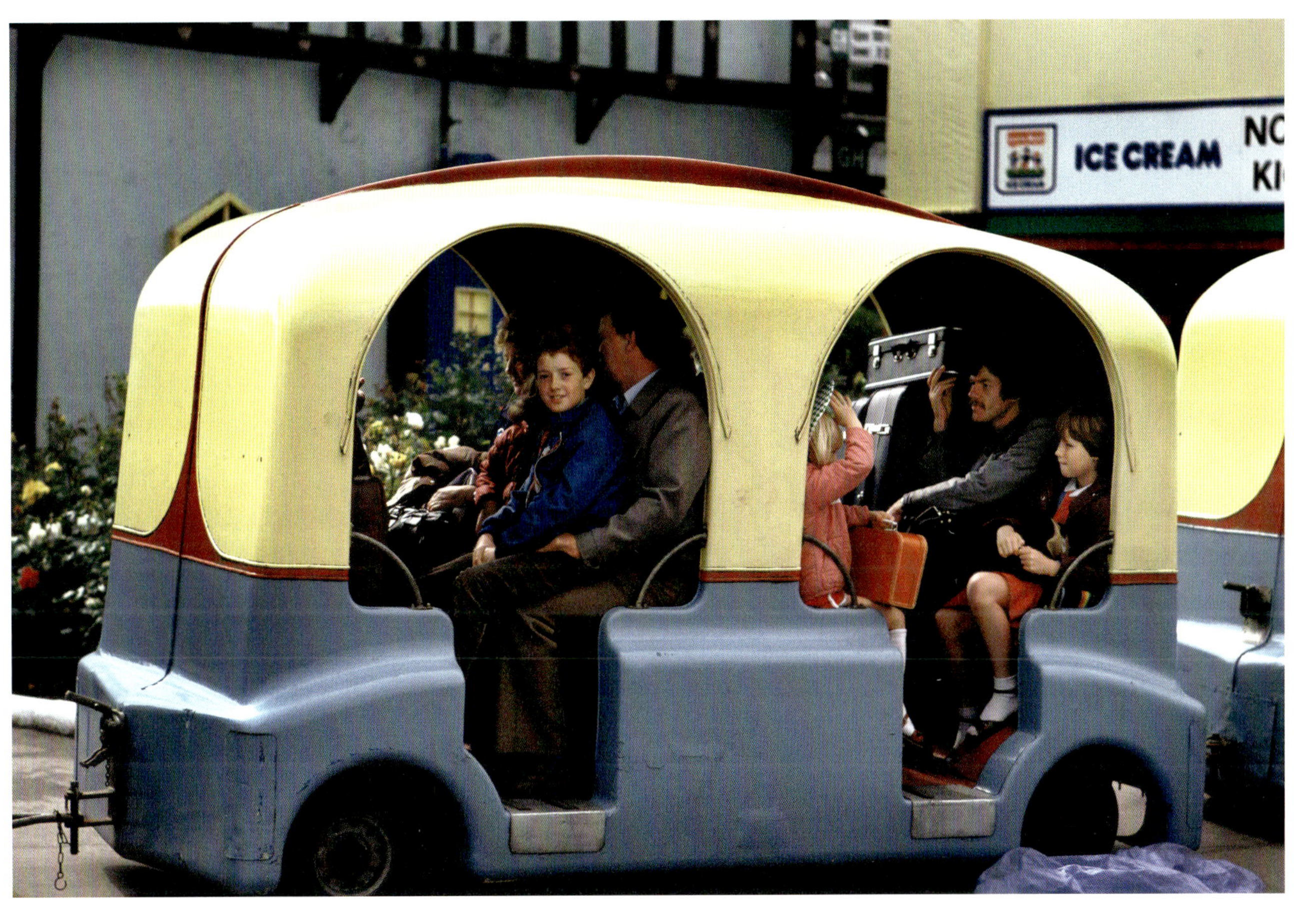

Campers and their luggage aboard a miniature train,
also known as the Butlinmobile, on the way to the chalets.

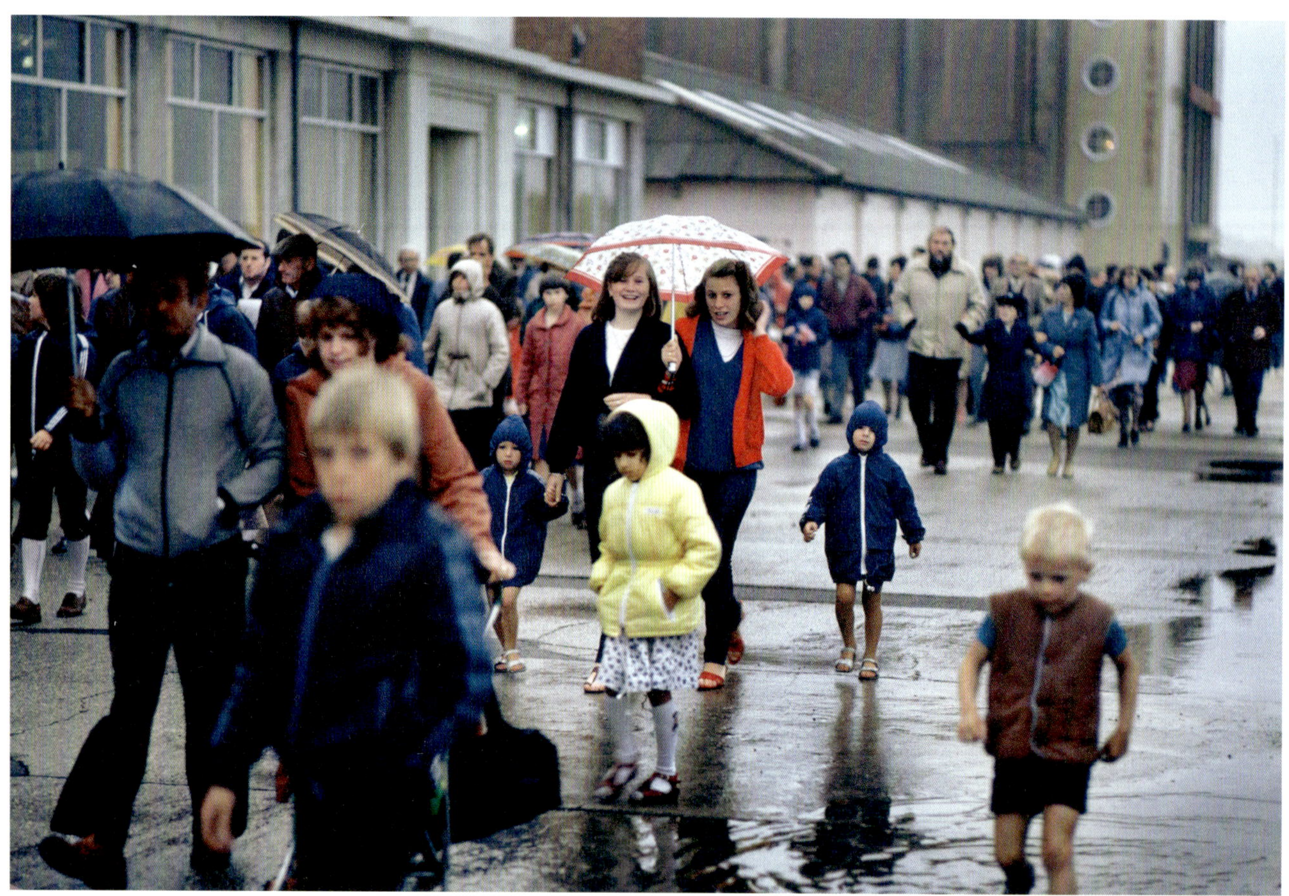

We caught a train, an early one
To Skegness by the sea
And now we're here at Butlin's
That's the place for you and me

Extract from 'Now We're at Butlin's', one of the many
songs holidaymakers were encouraged to sing in the camp
along with the Redcoats (entertainment staff)

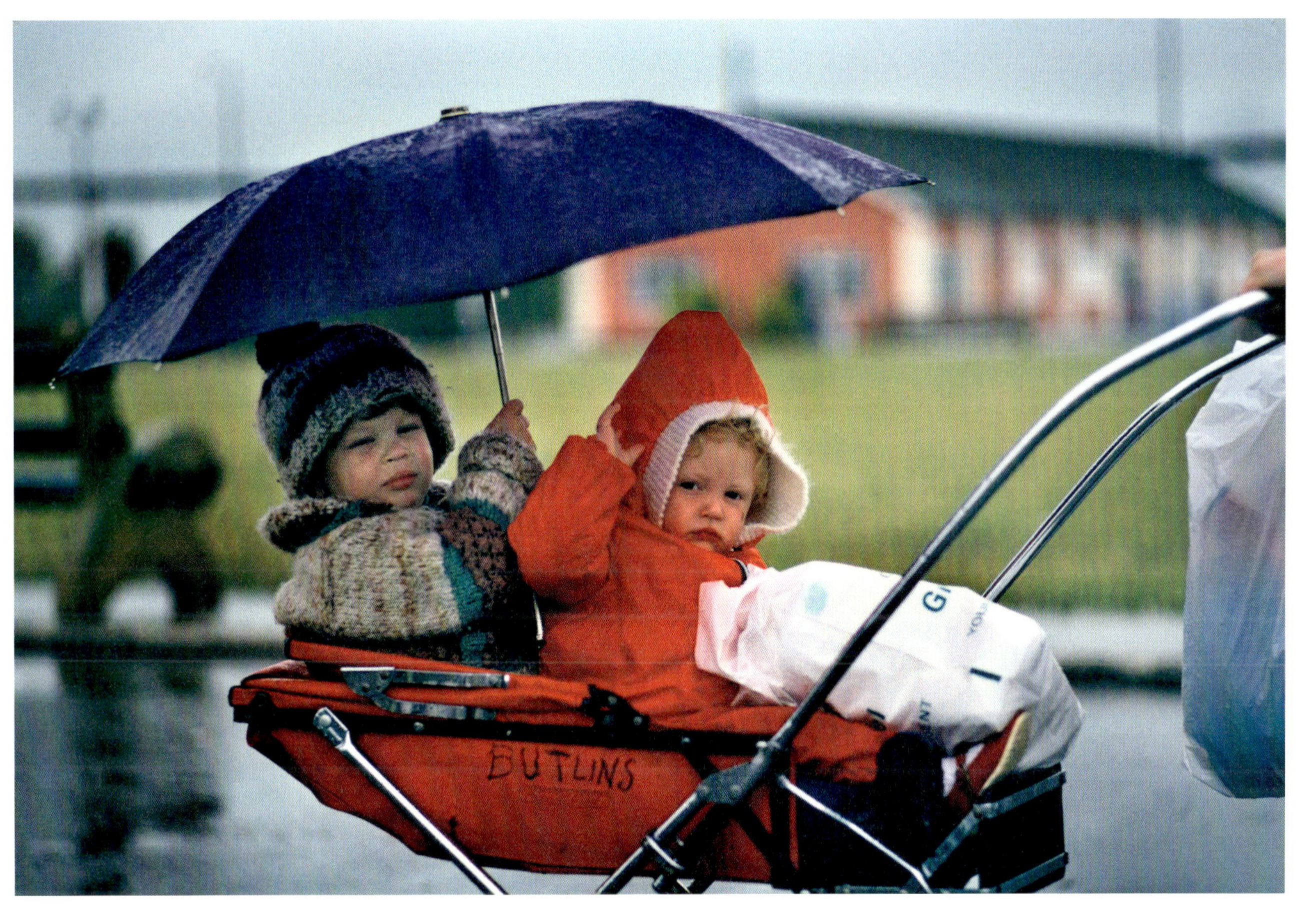

Pram hire, trained nurses and day crèches:
infants' needs were all catered for at Butlin's.

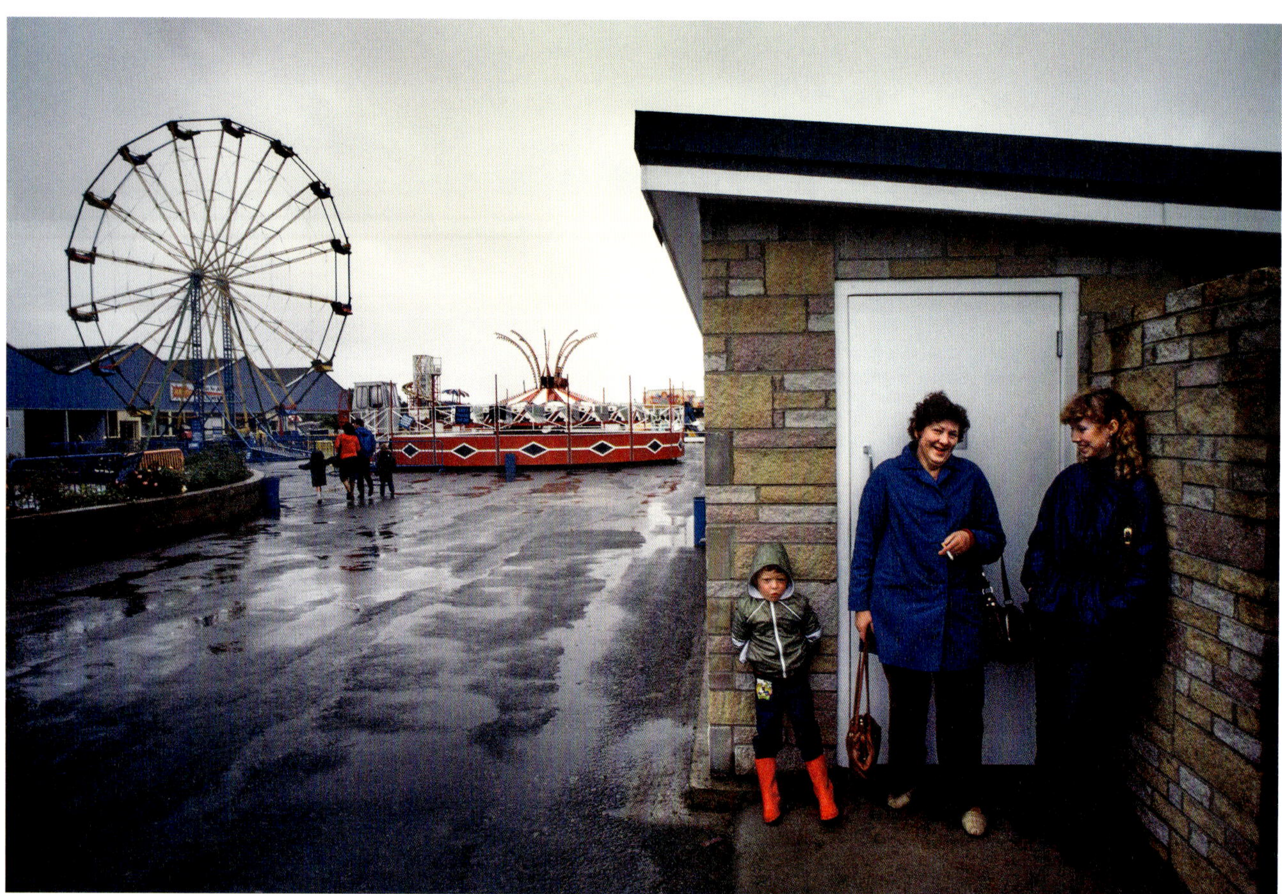

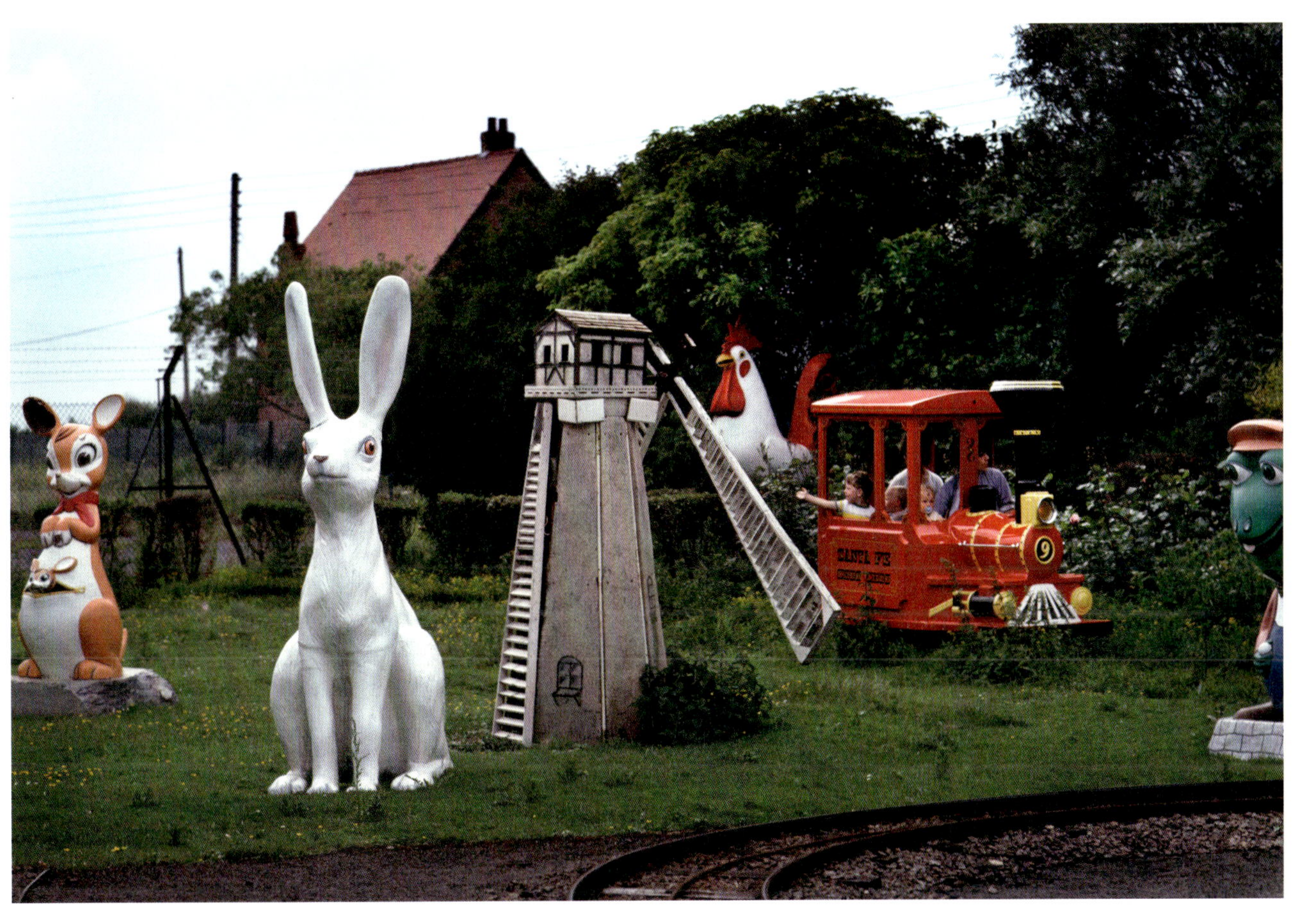

When the rain stopped children from playing in the fairground
there was always a ride on the miniature railway.

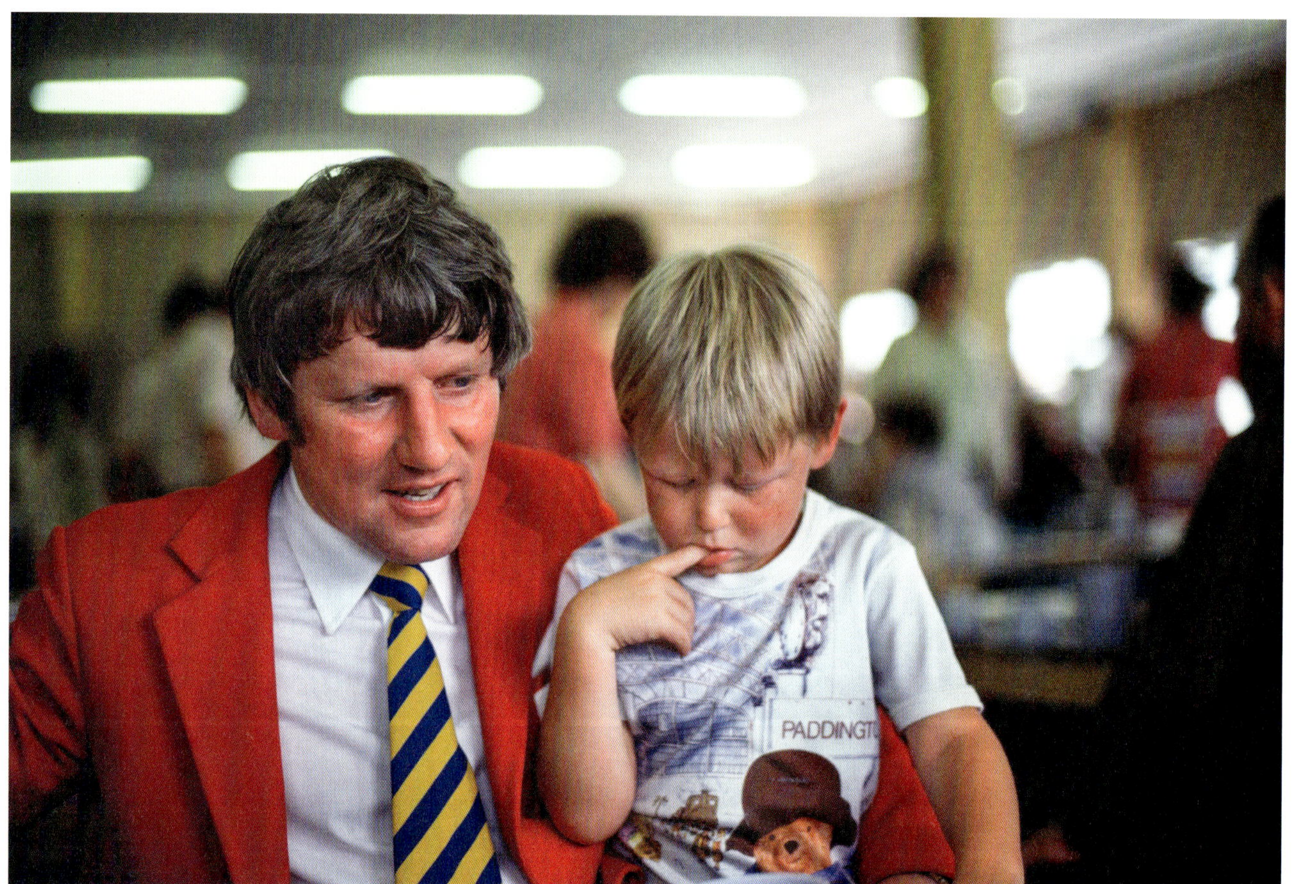
PADDINGT

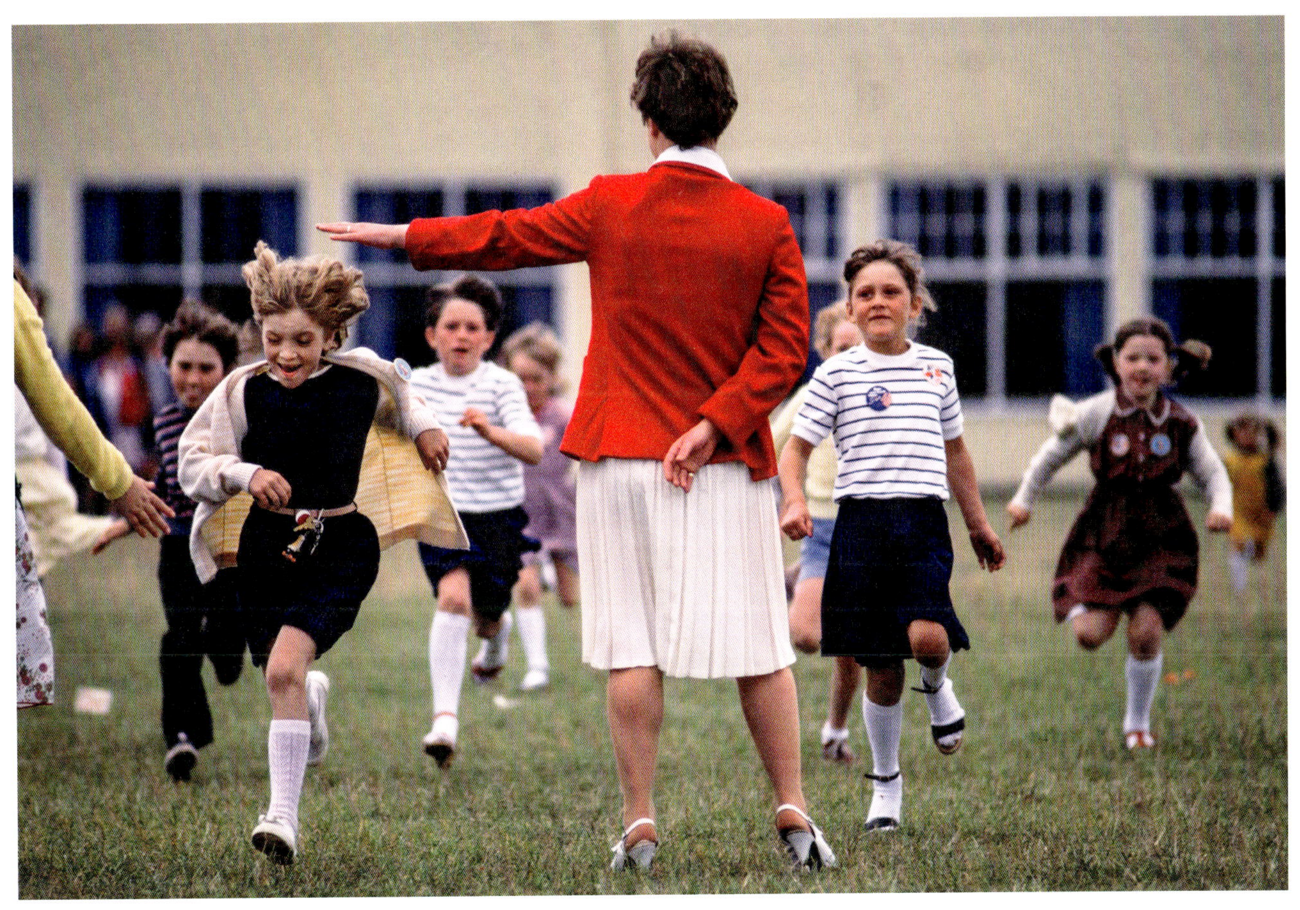

The Redcoats ran the kids' clubs,
giving parents time to relax elsewhere.

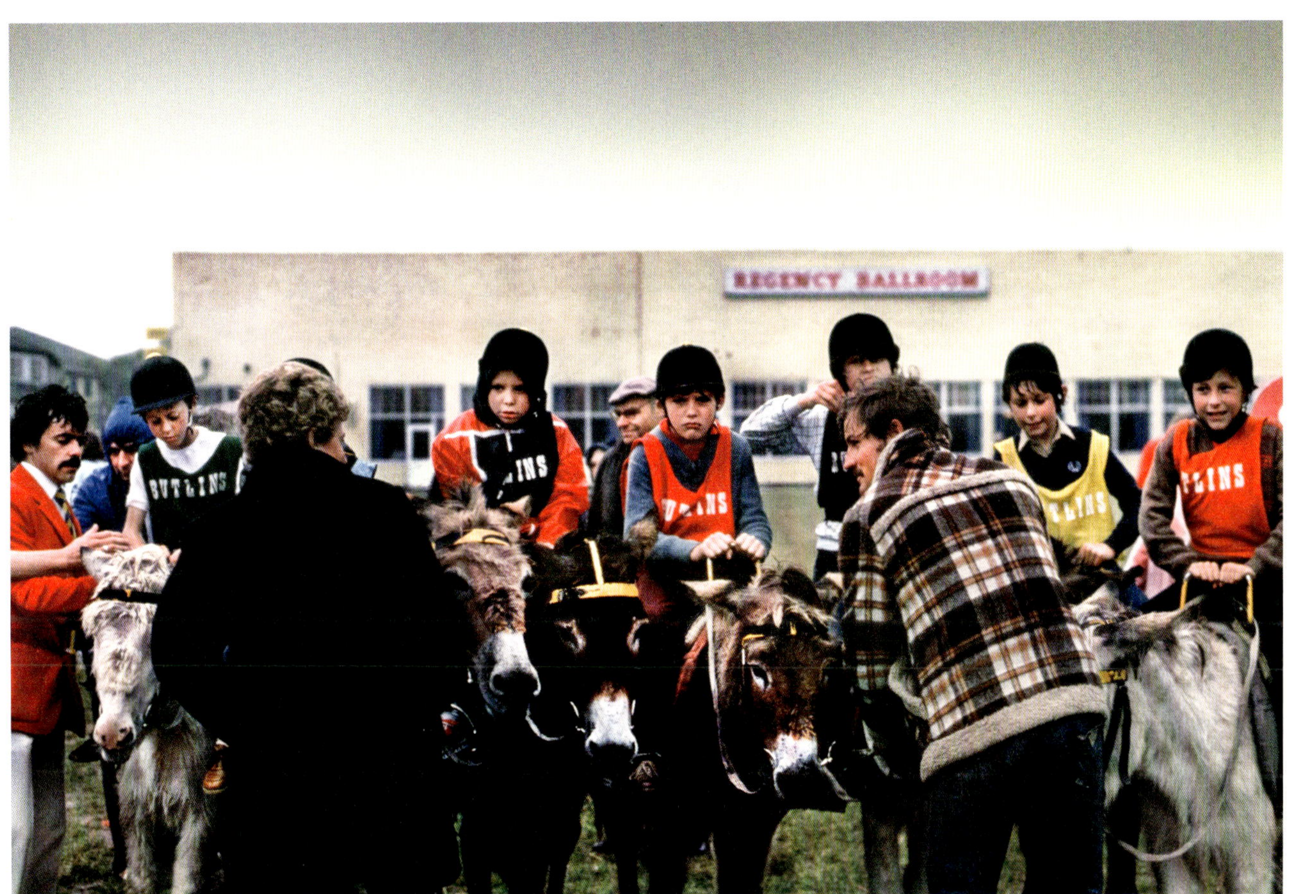

The final of the donkey derby. The race was a nod to traditional horse racing but guests could only bet with token amounts.

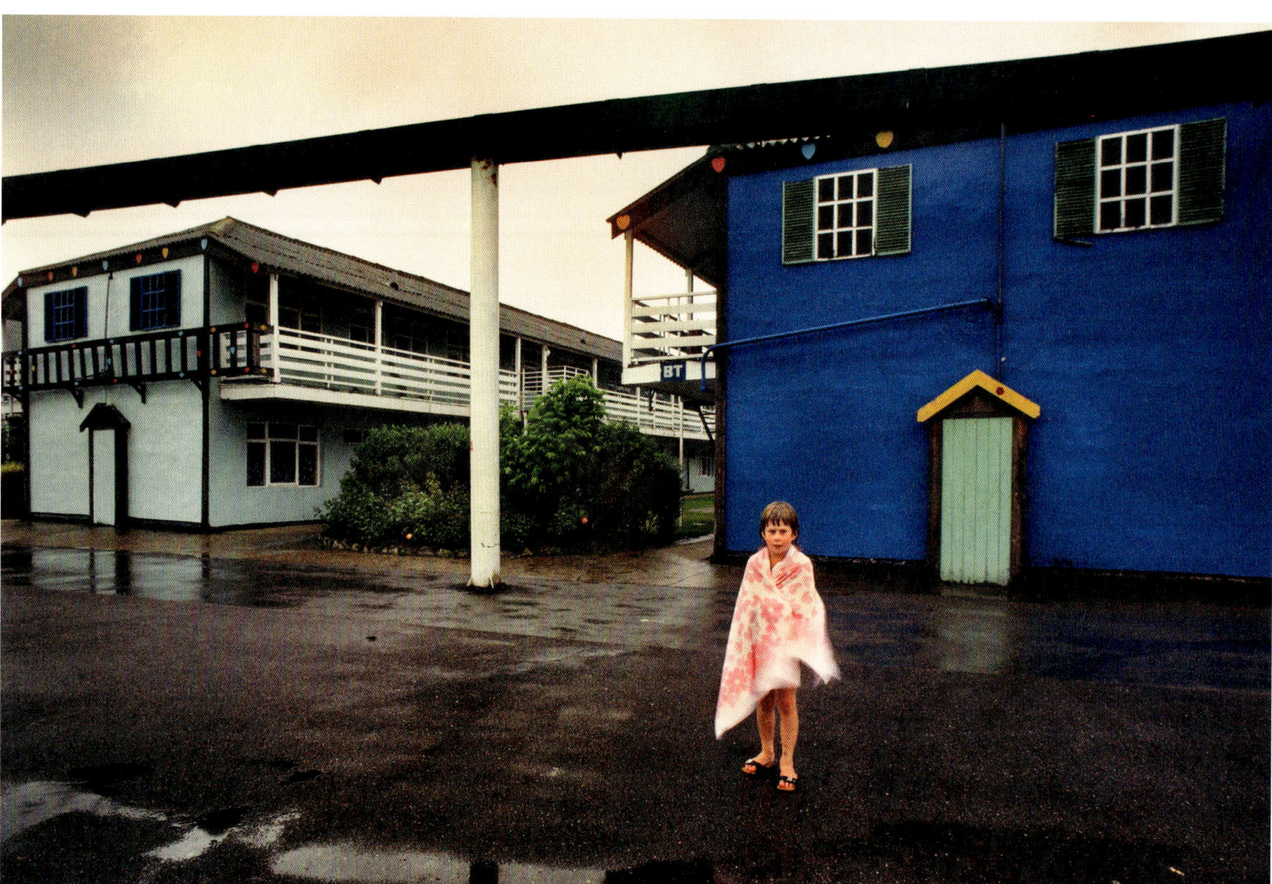

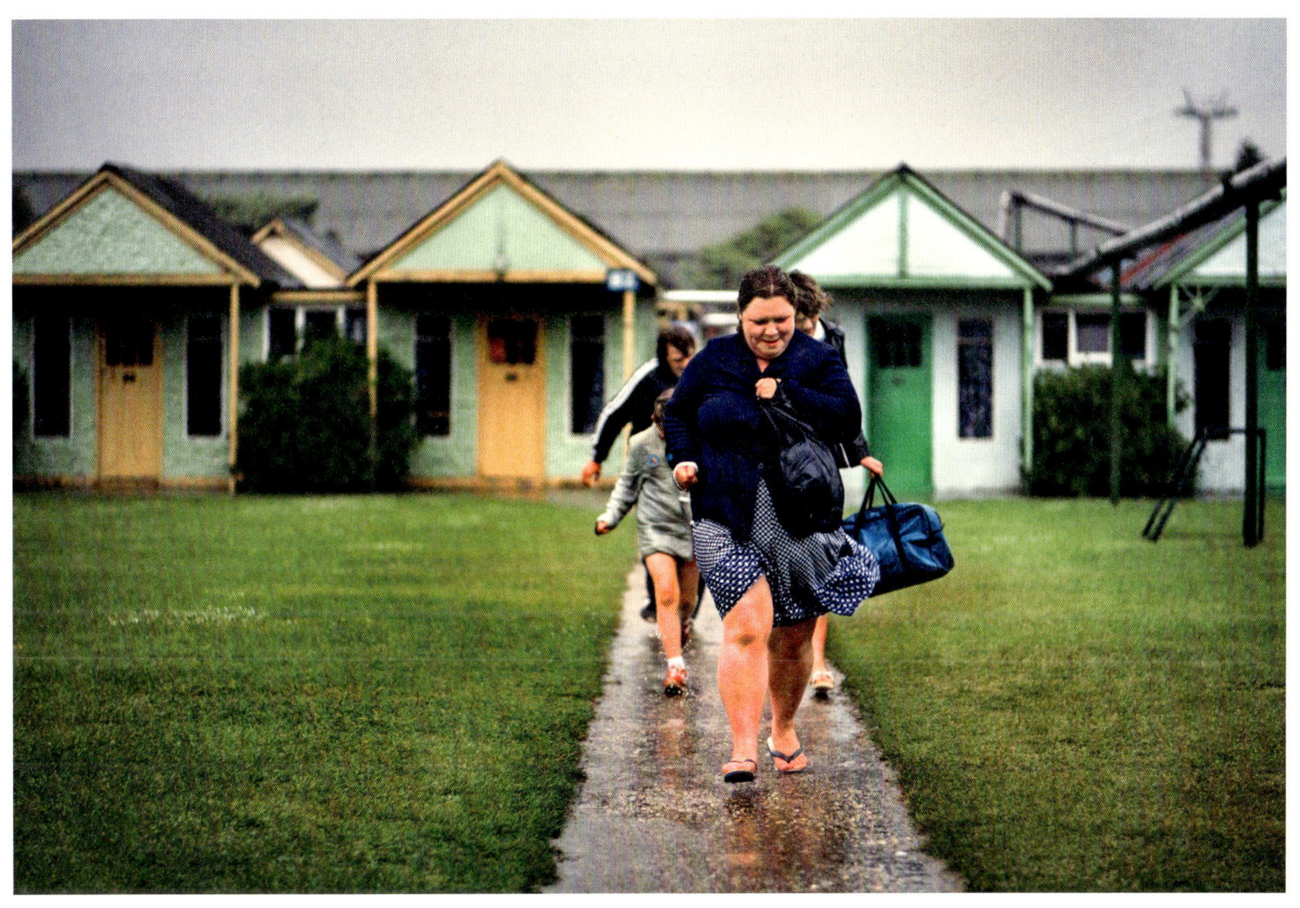

Swimming in the rain: despite the unpredictable
British weather, campers made the best of it.

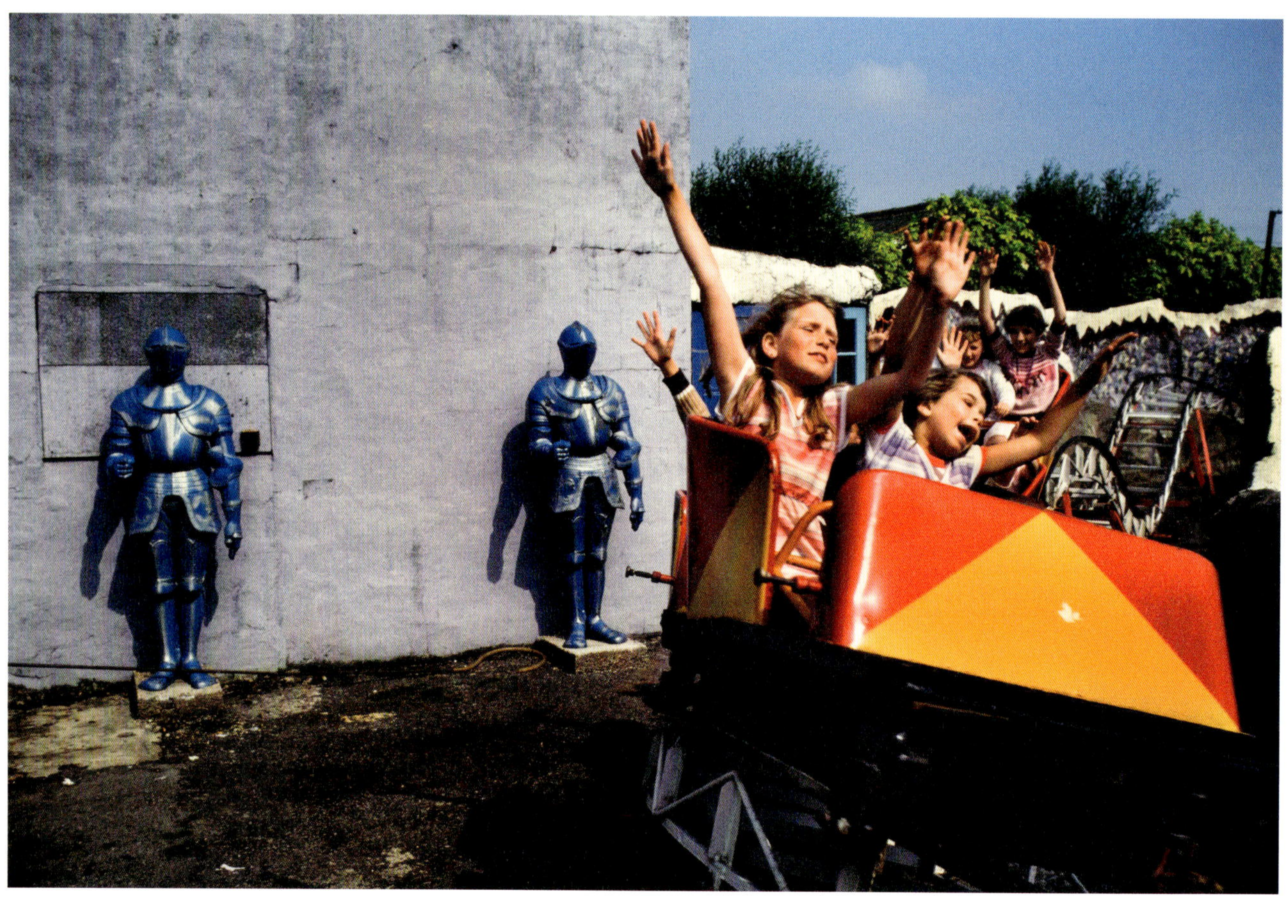

When things are looking gloomy
And skies are dull and grey
Remember that the sun will come
And shine another day
So open up your faces wide
And let me hear you say
Hi-De-Hi, Hi-De-Ho!

Extract from the song 'Hi-De-Hi'

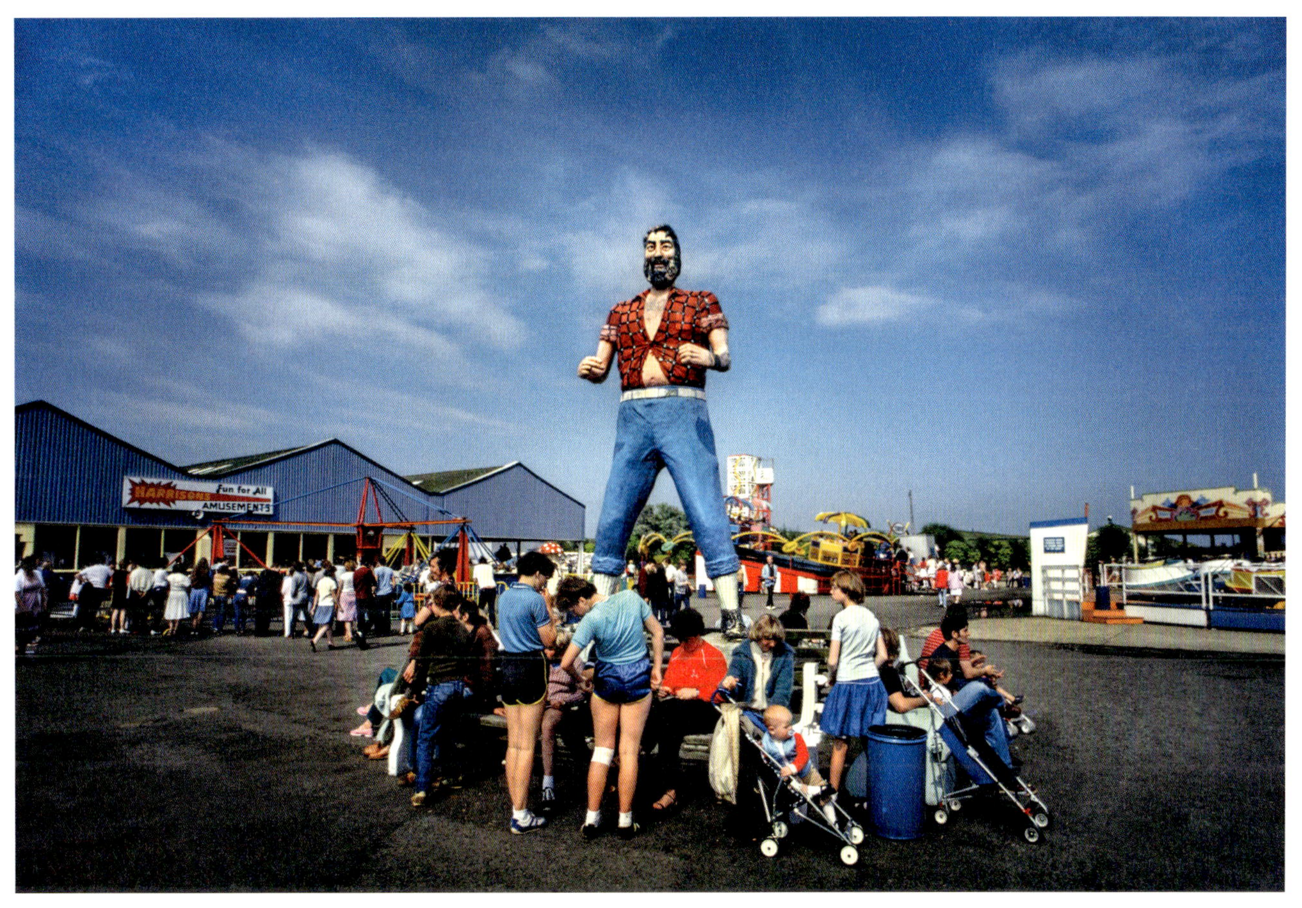

The Skegness Giant was a popular meeting
point in the centre of the camp.

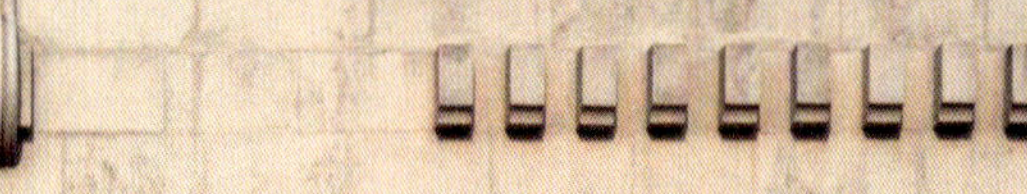
BUTLINS

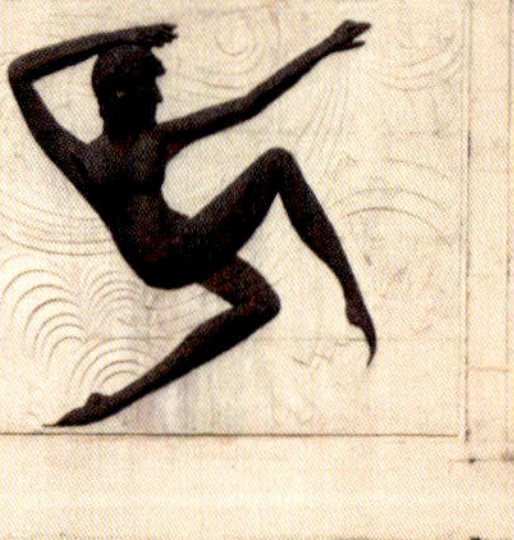

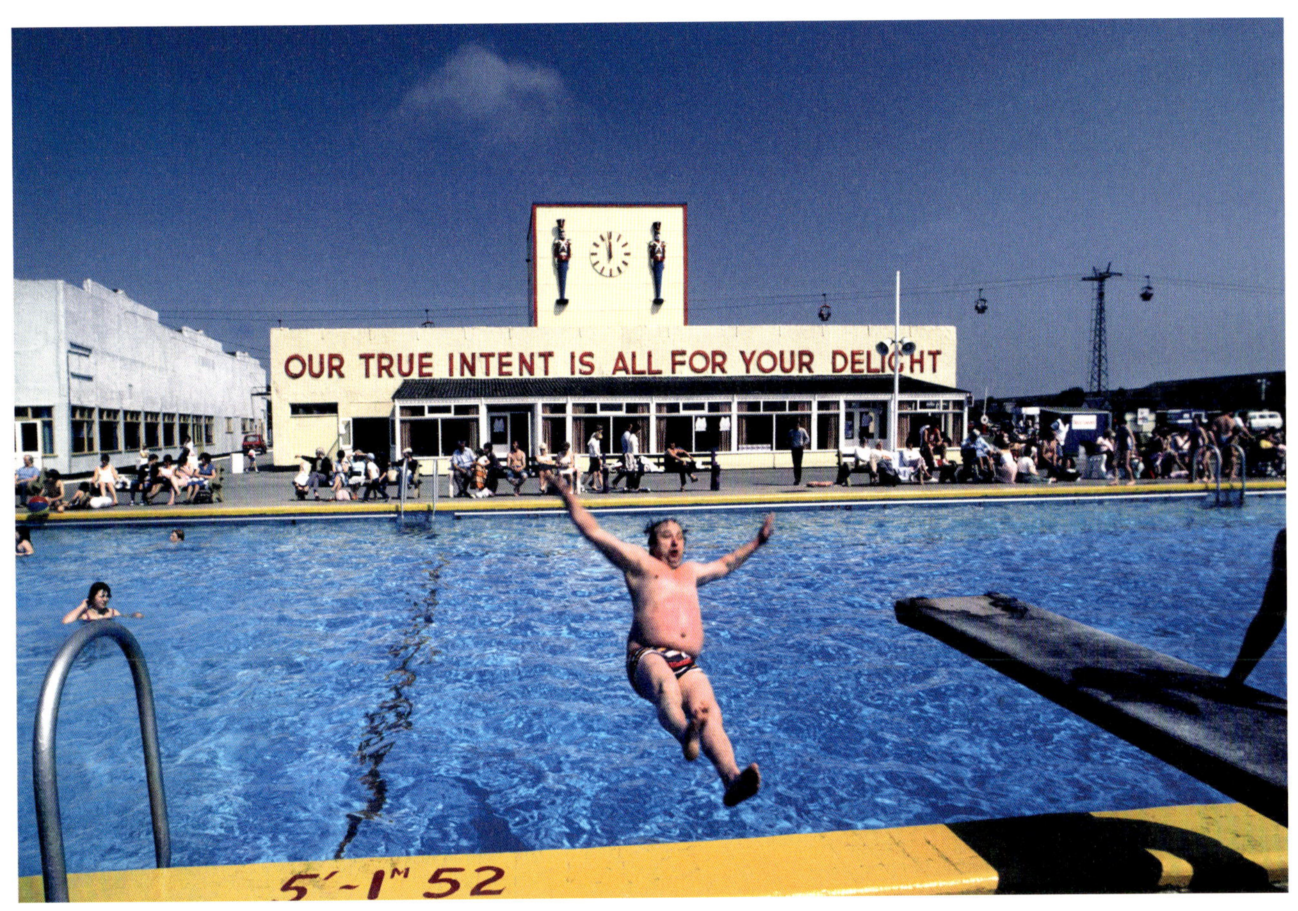

The original art deco reception and swimming pool were built
for the opening of the Skegness camp in 1936.

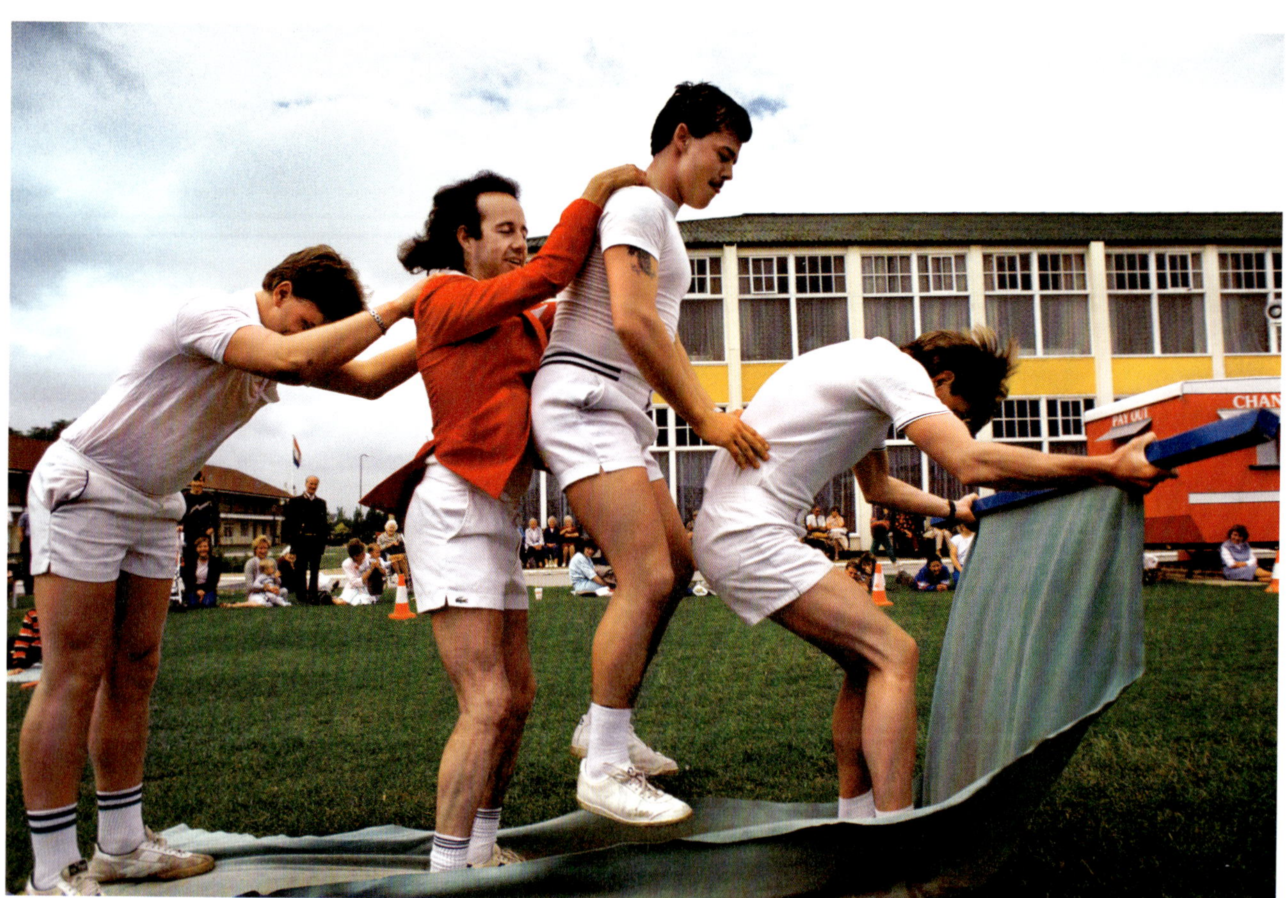

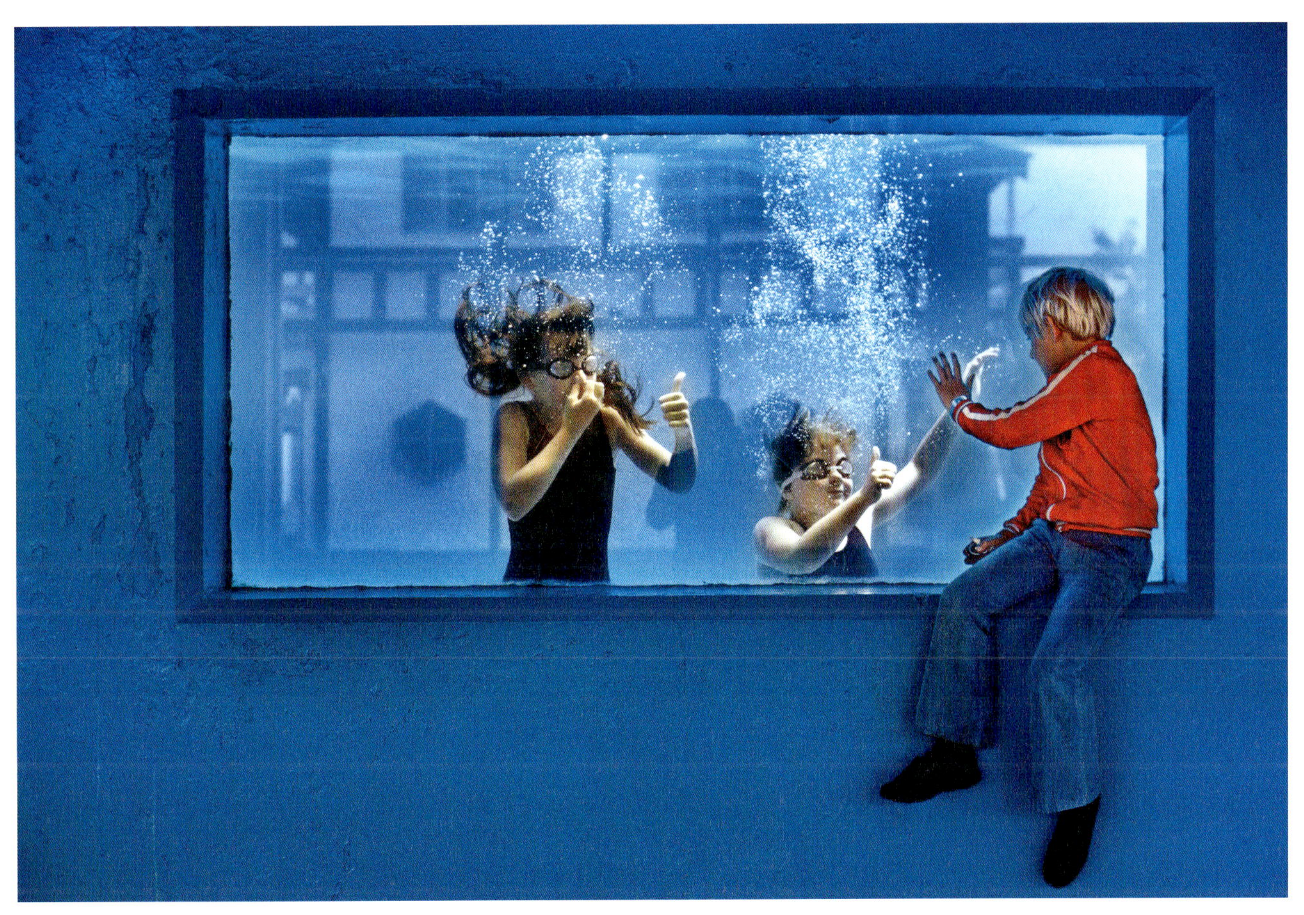

Activities were playful and varied, ranging from group sports days to the famous human aquarium.

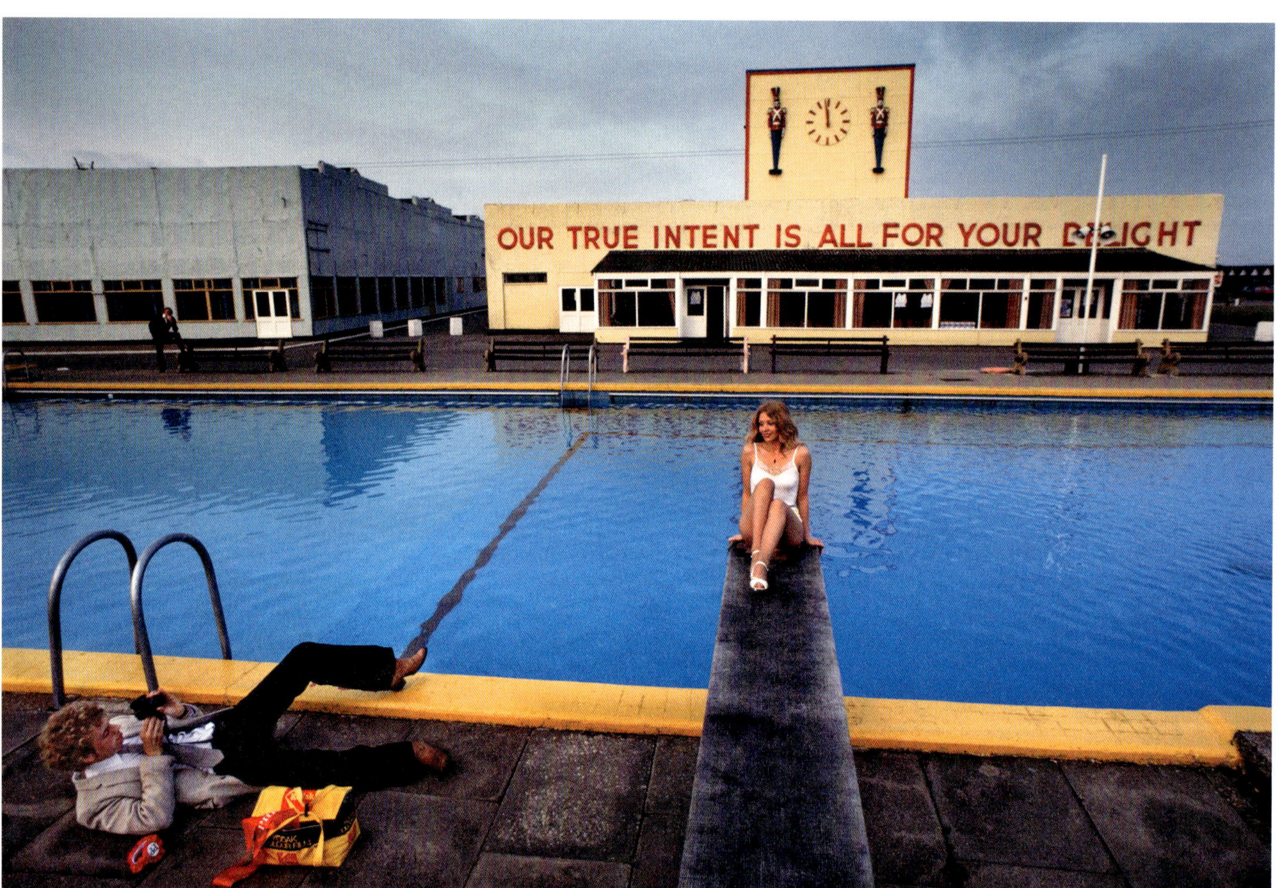
OUR TRUE INTENT IS ALL FOR YOUR DELIGHT

**We swim and dance
And find romance
A holiday at Butlin's
The friendships made
Will never fade
A holiday at Butlin's**

Extract from the song 'A Holiday at Butlin's'

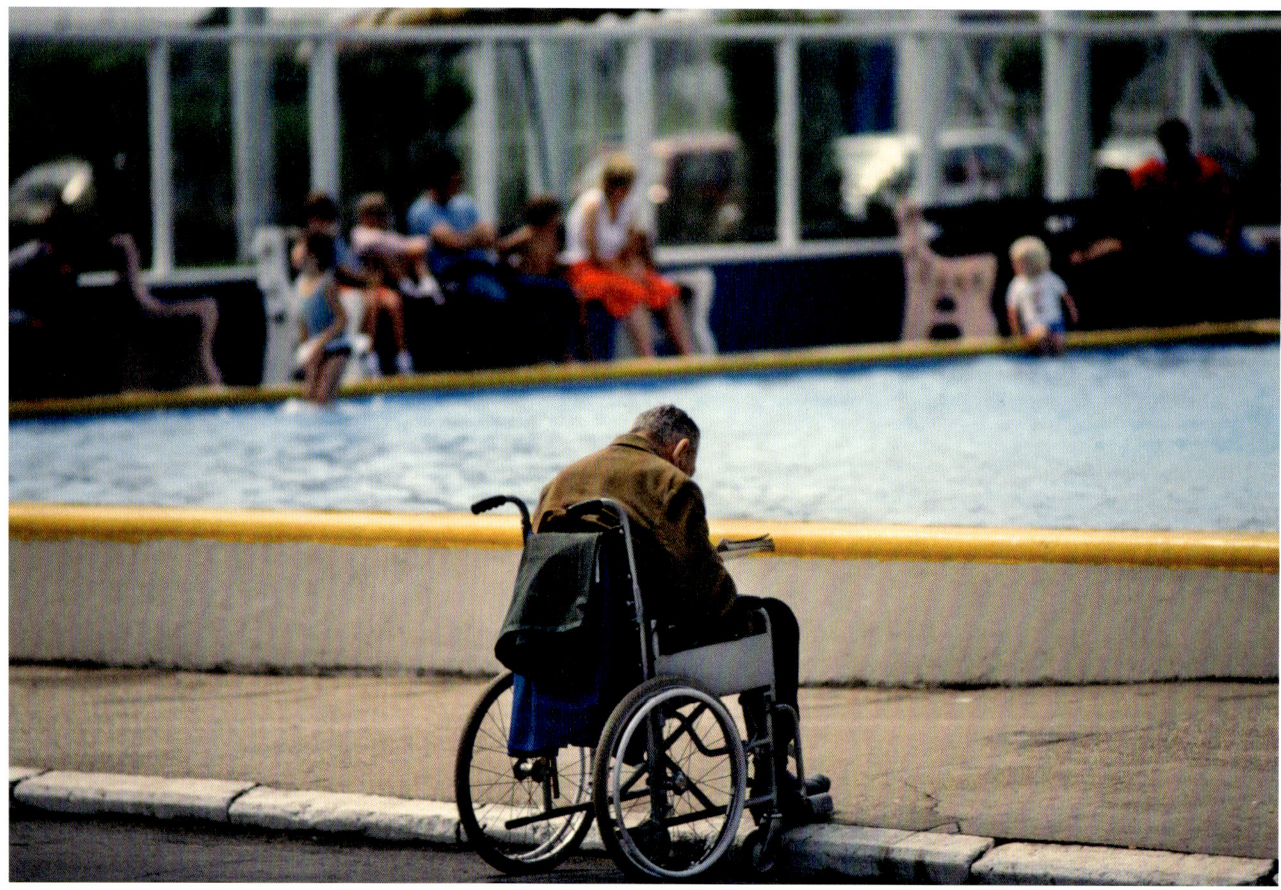

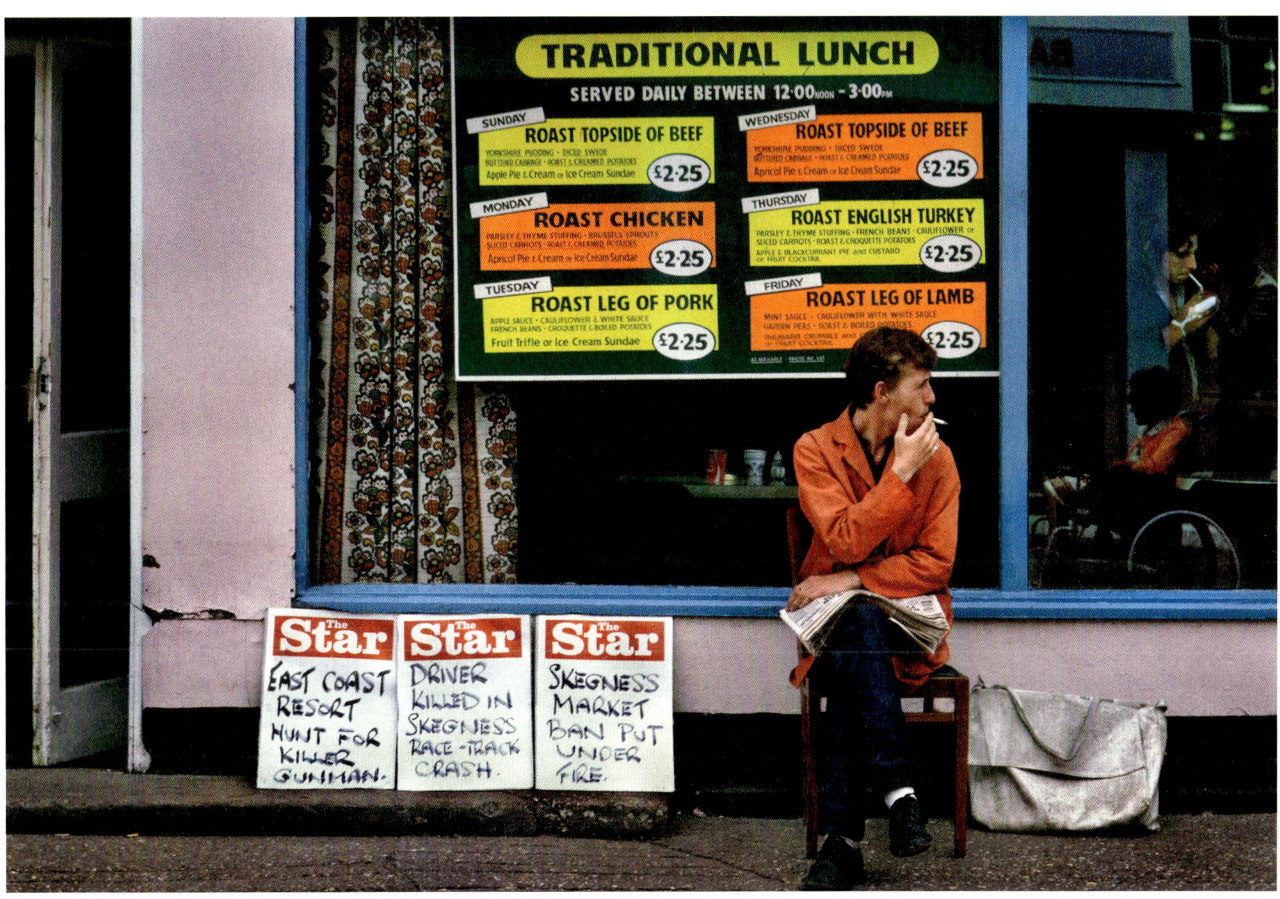

Among the crowds of visitors, individuals still
had space and time for quiet moments.

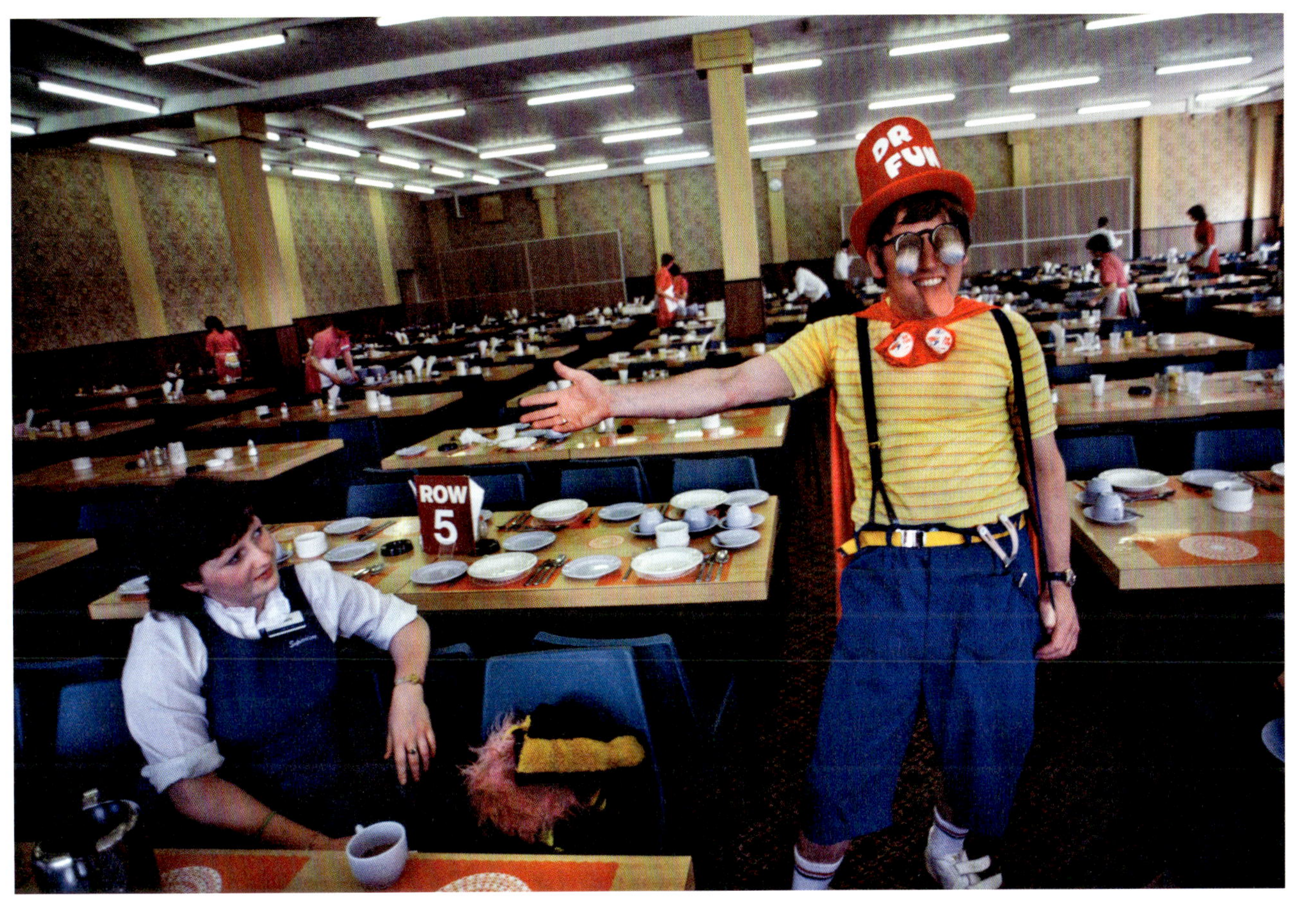

Dr Fun, a Redcoat, in the Lincoln Dining Room, where
more than 10,000 meals were served each day.

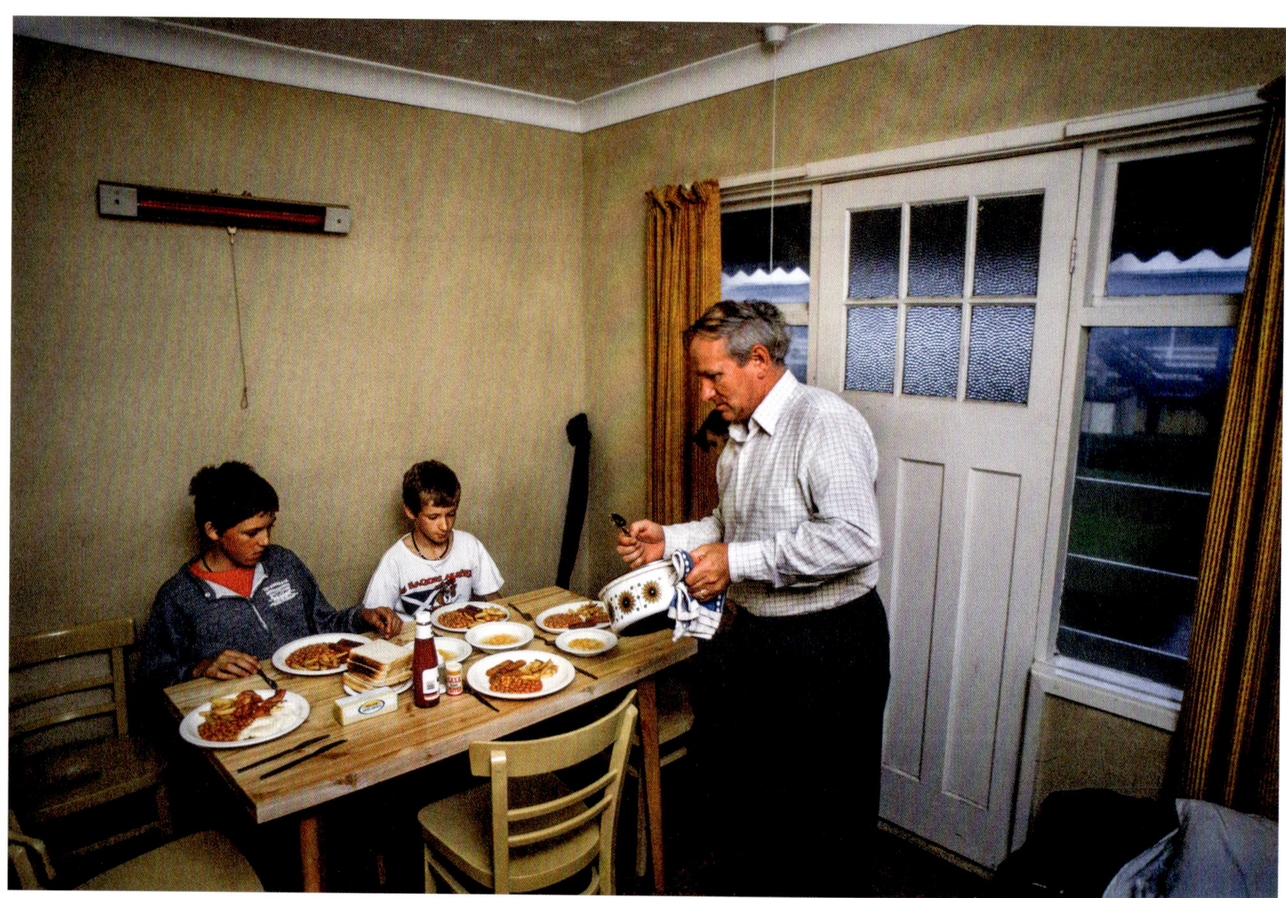

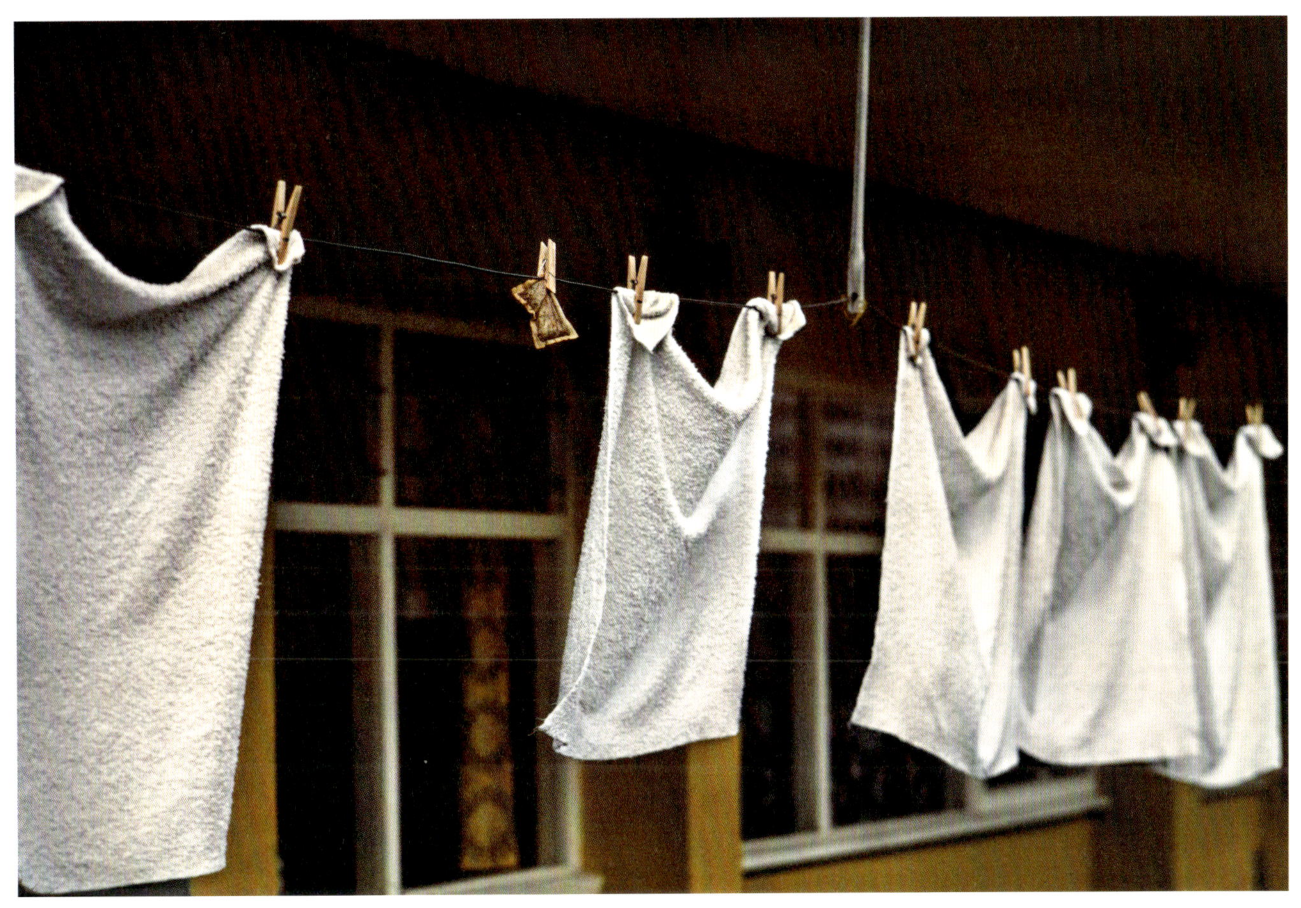

Self-catering was introduced in the 70s by Billy Butlin's son, Bobby.
Outside, terry nappies (and a teabag) were left to dry.

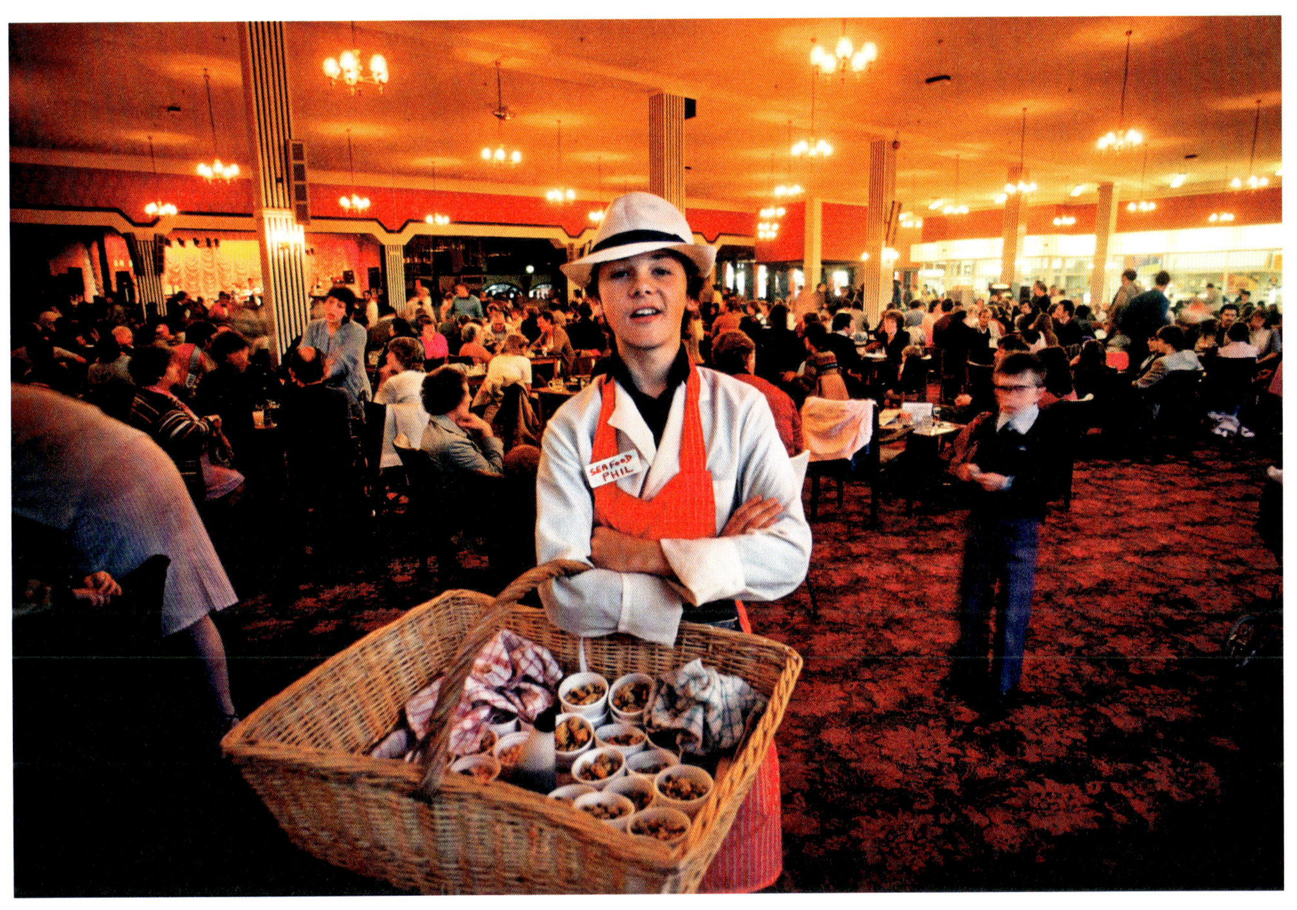

Seafood Phil, a local boy, selling fresh cockles
and mussels in the Regency Bar.

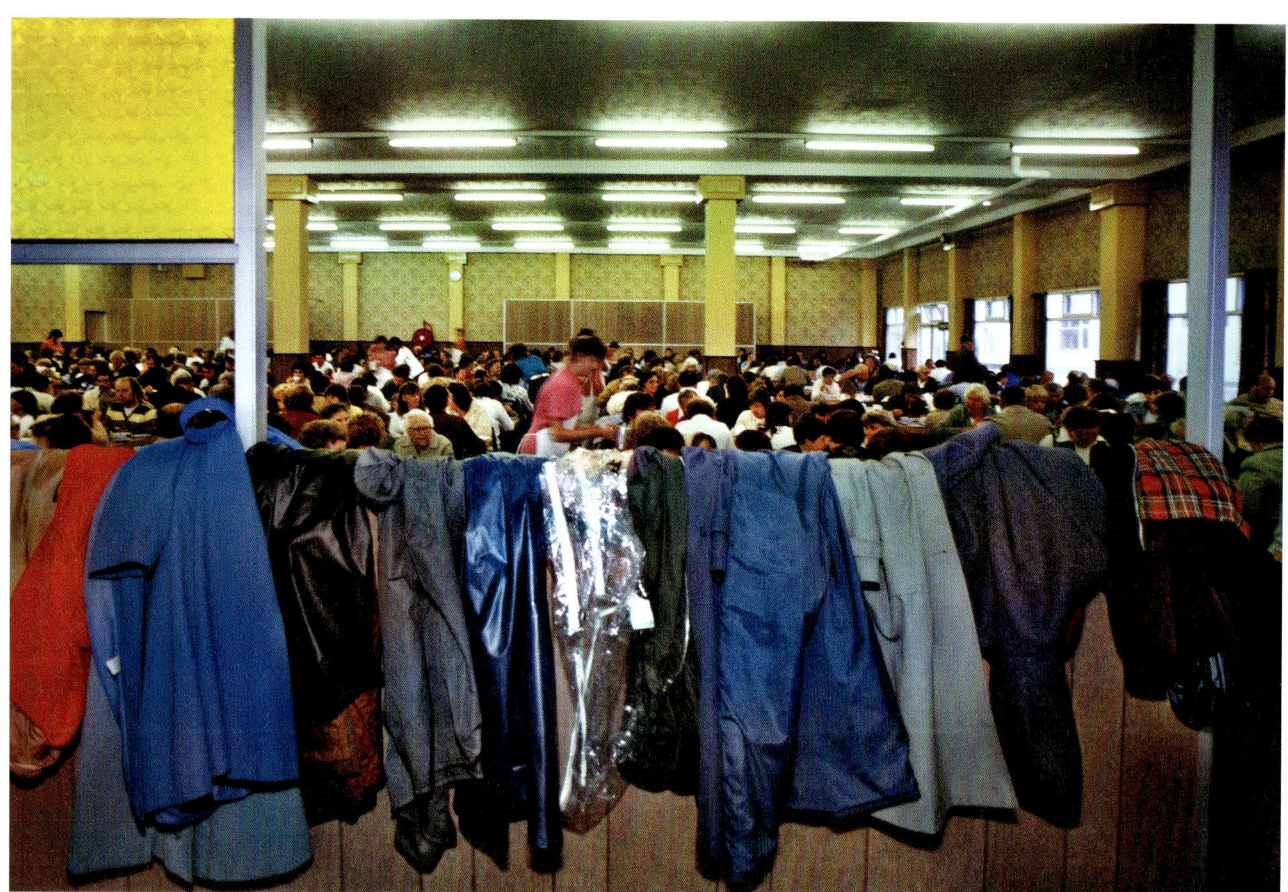

5.5 million eggs

100 tons of sausages (would stretch for 217 miles)

120,000 gallons of soup (enough for 4 million portions)

1,570 tons of potatoes (216 acres of crops)

34 tons of tea (enough for over 20 million cups)

240 tons of pork chops (requiring over 8,000 pigs!)

Butlin's food shopping list for an average year, published in 1961

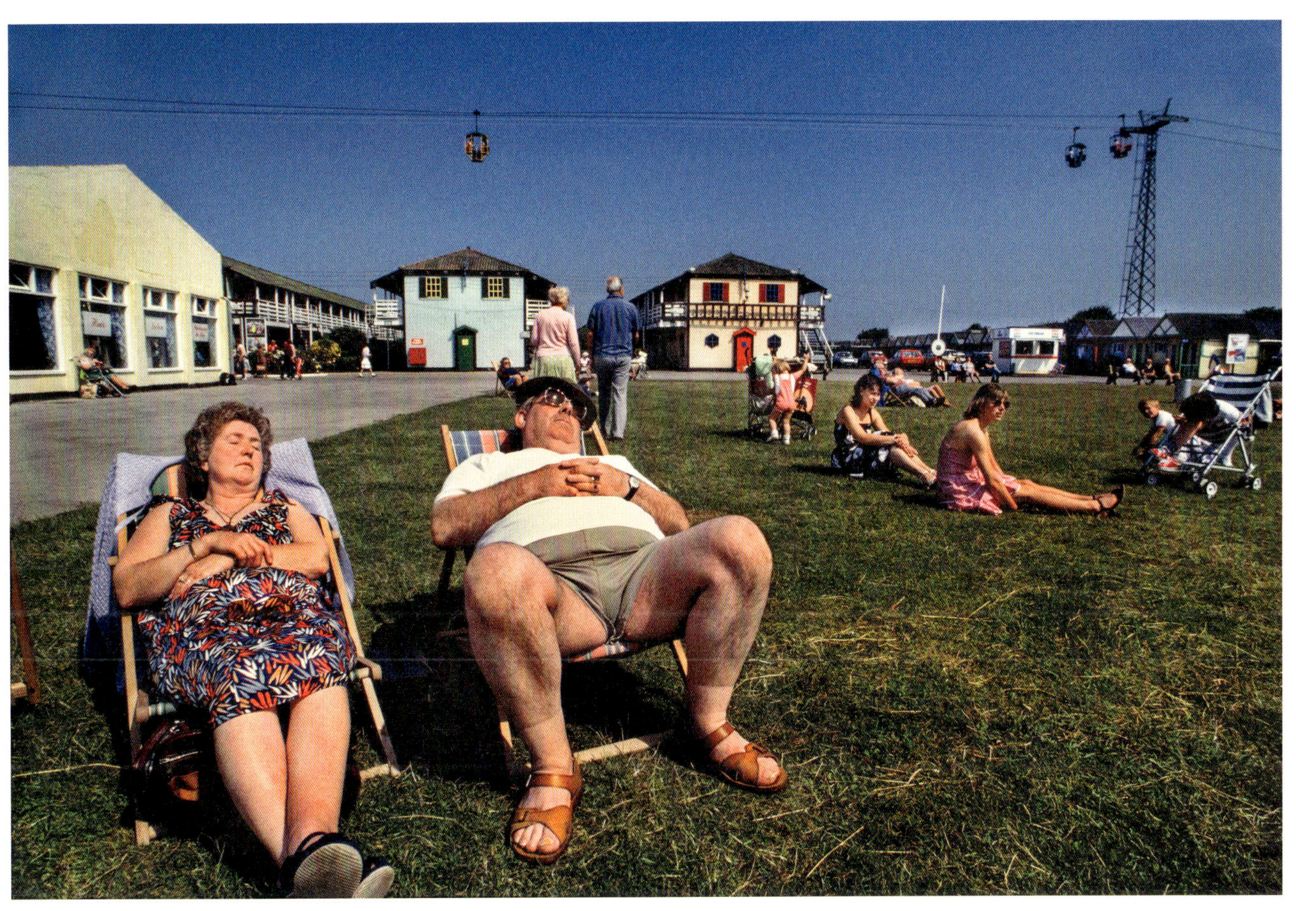

Campers relaxing on the sports field on a warm
afternoon while a chairlift passes overhead.

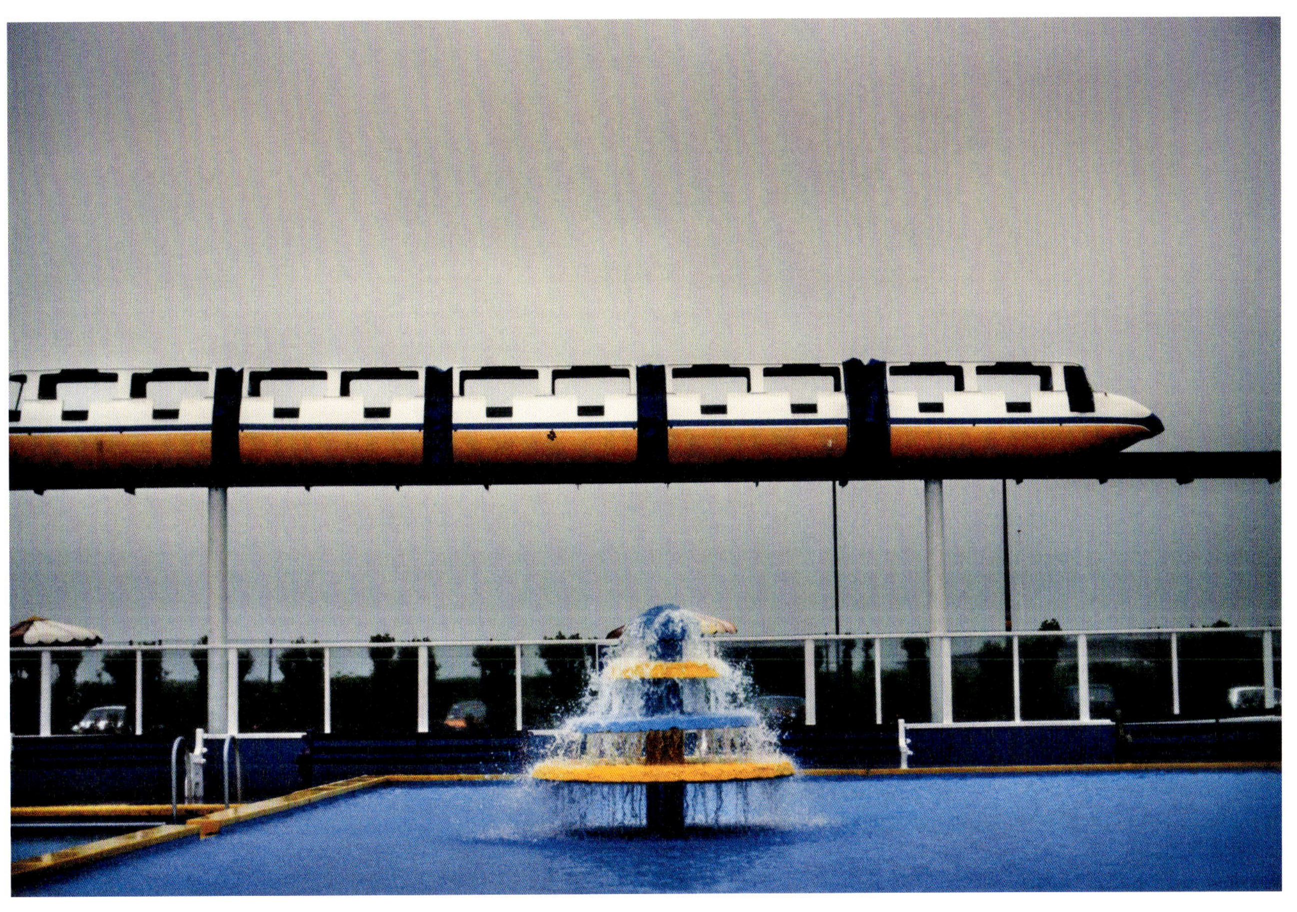

The UK's first commercial monorail, built as a
pleasure ride for the Skegness camp in 1965.

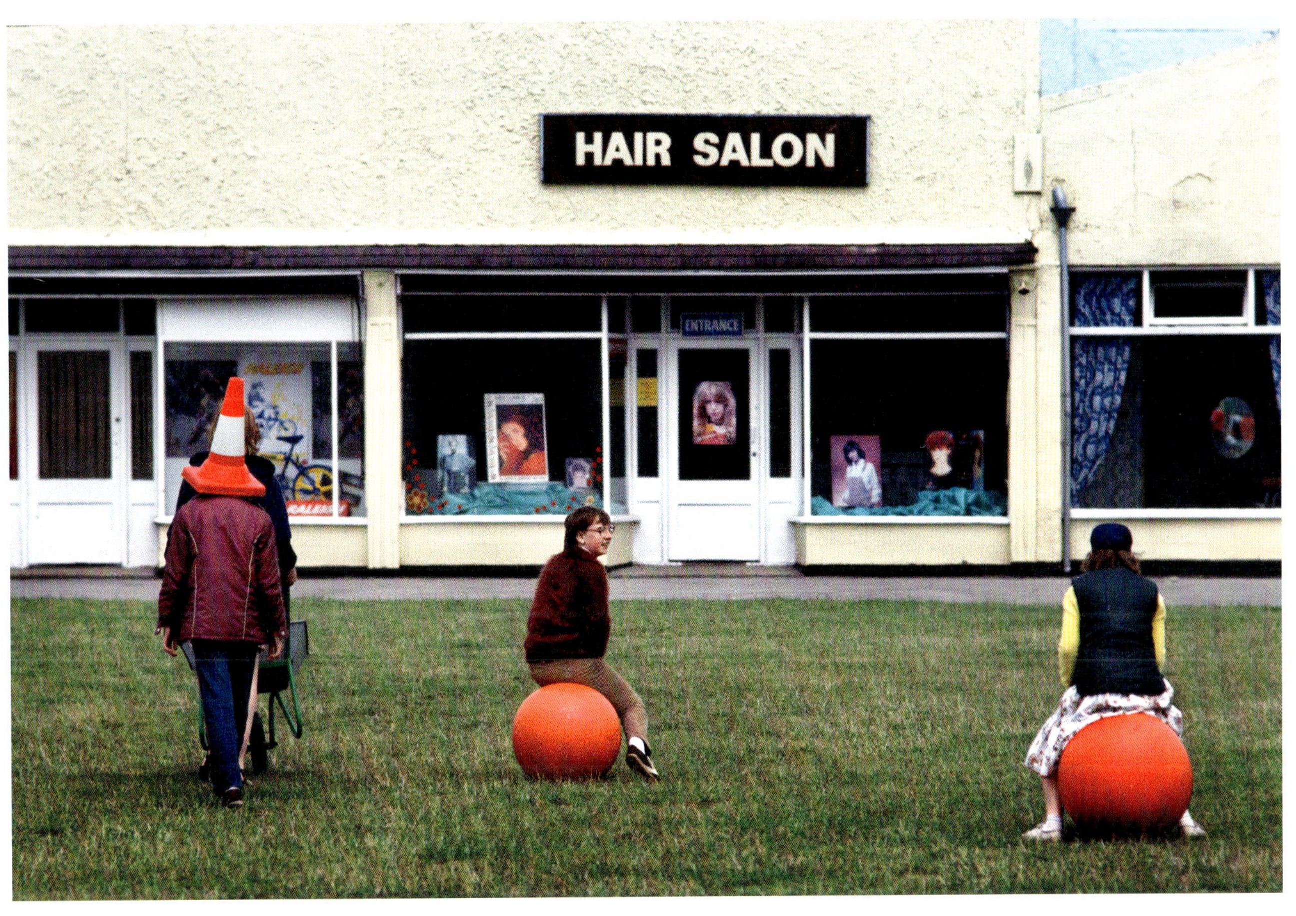

Contestants leaving the sports field after
the space hopper championship.

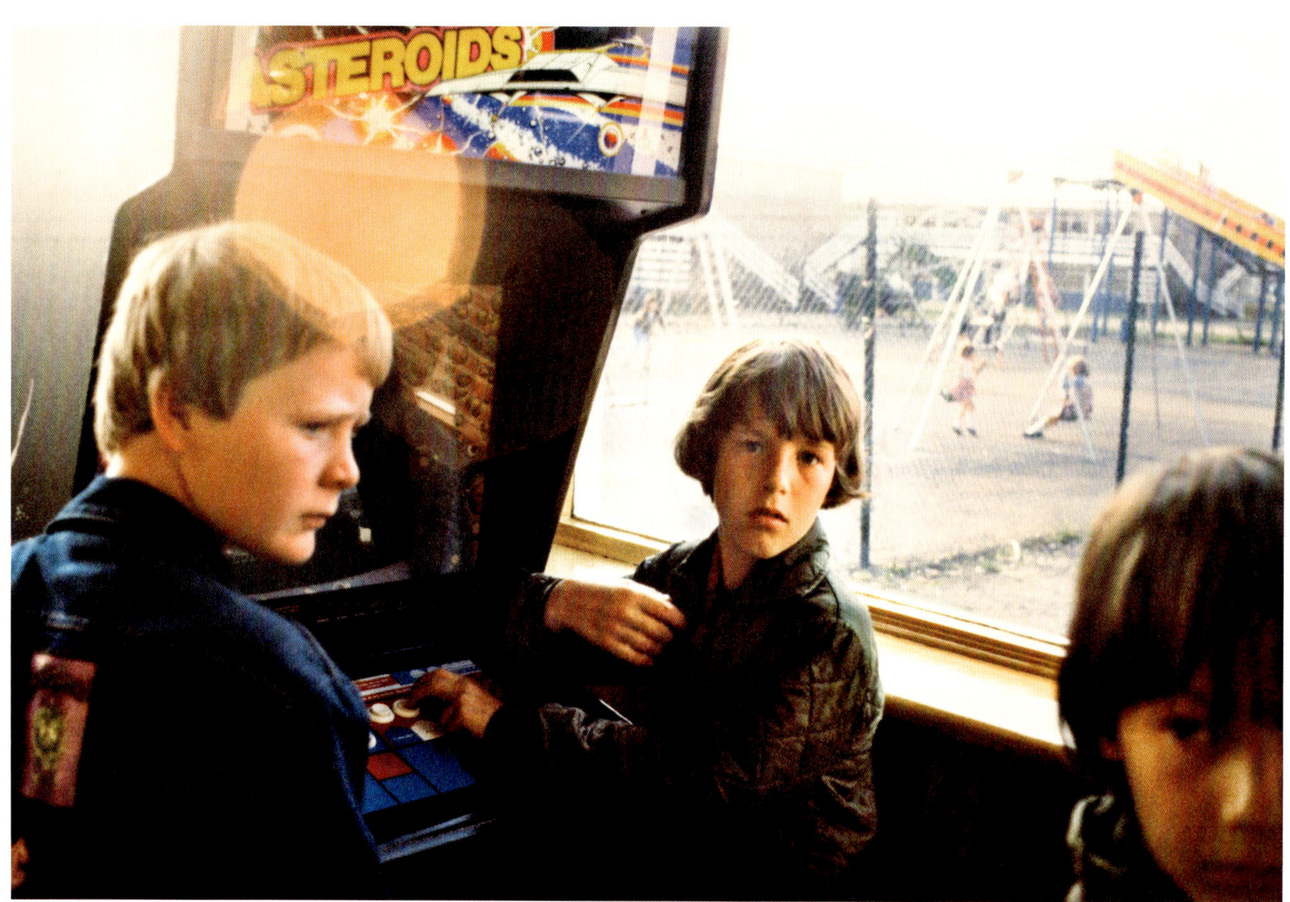
STEROIDS

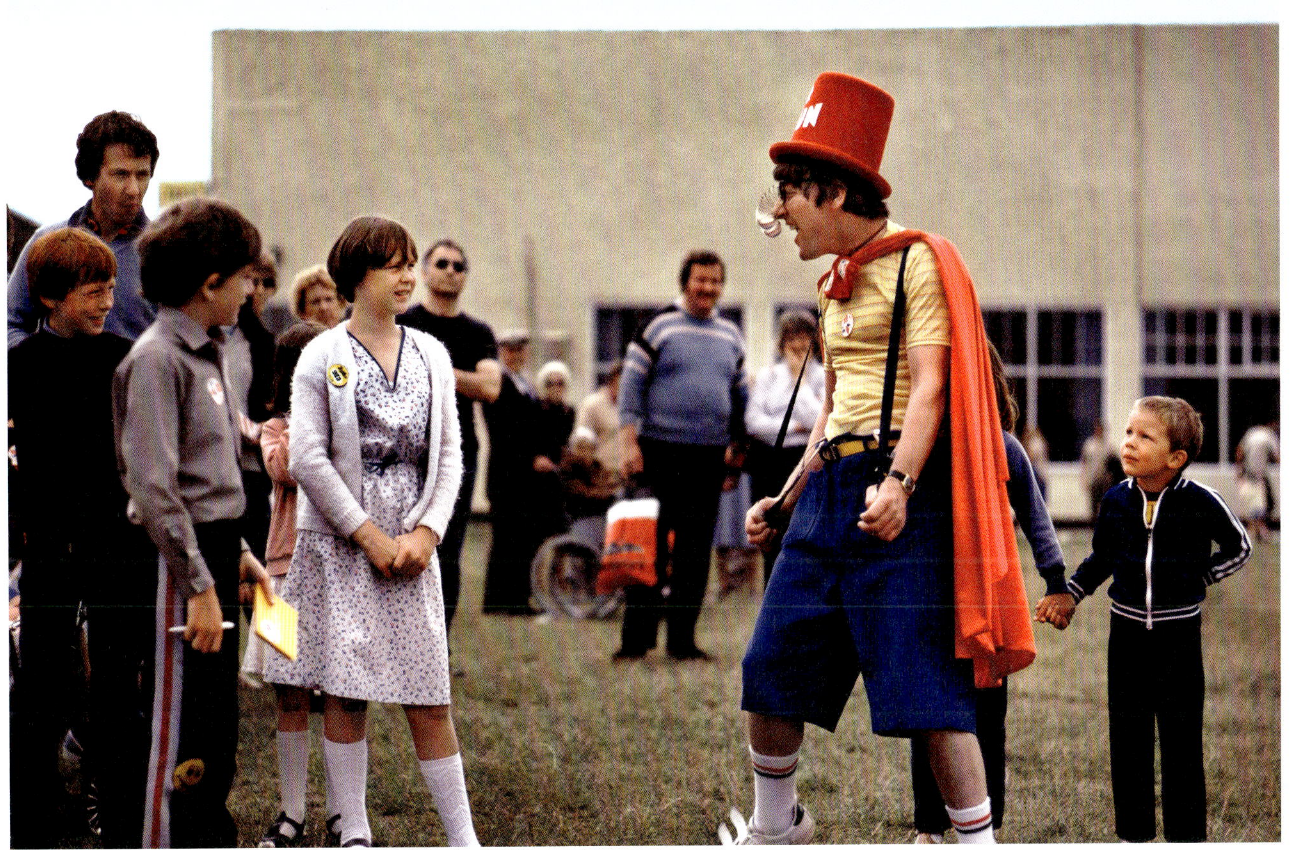

Young boys play arcade games while Dr Fun
entertains the families outside.

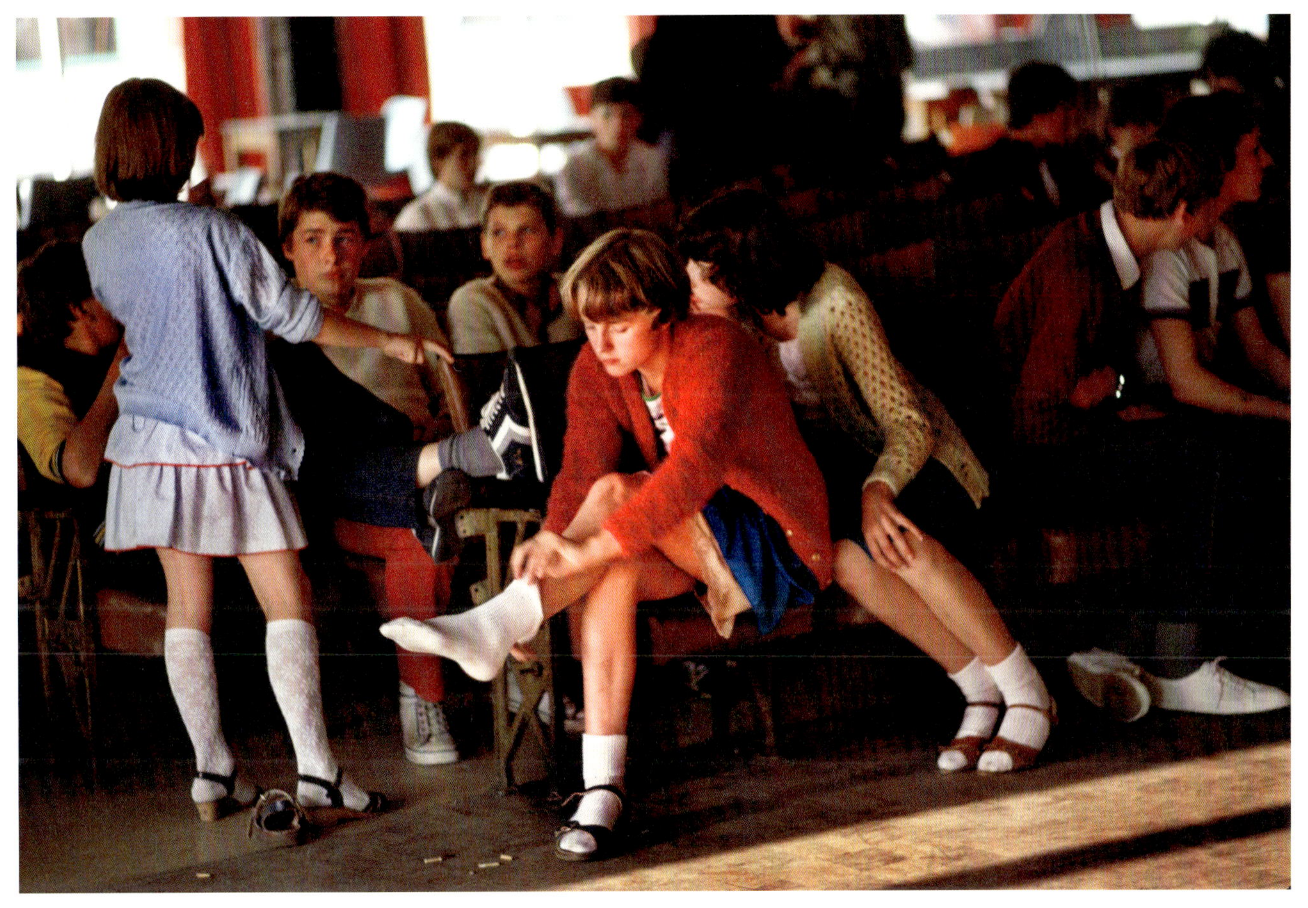

Teenagers hanging out for the afternoon in the Empress Ballroom
before the start of the evening entertainment.

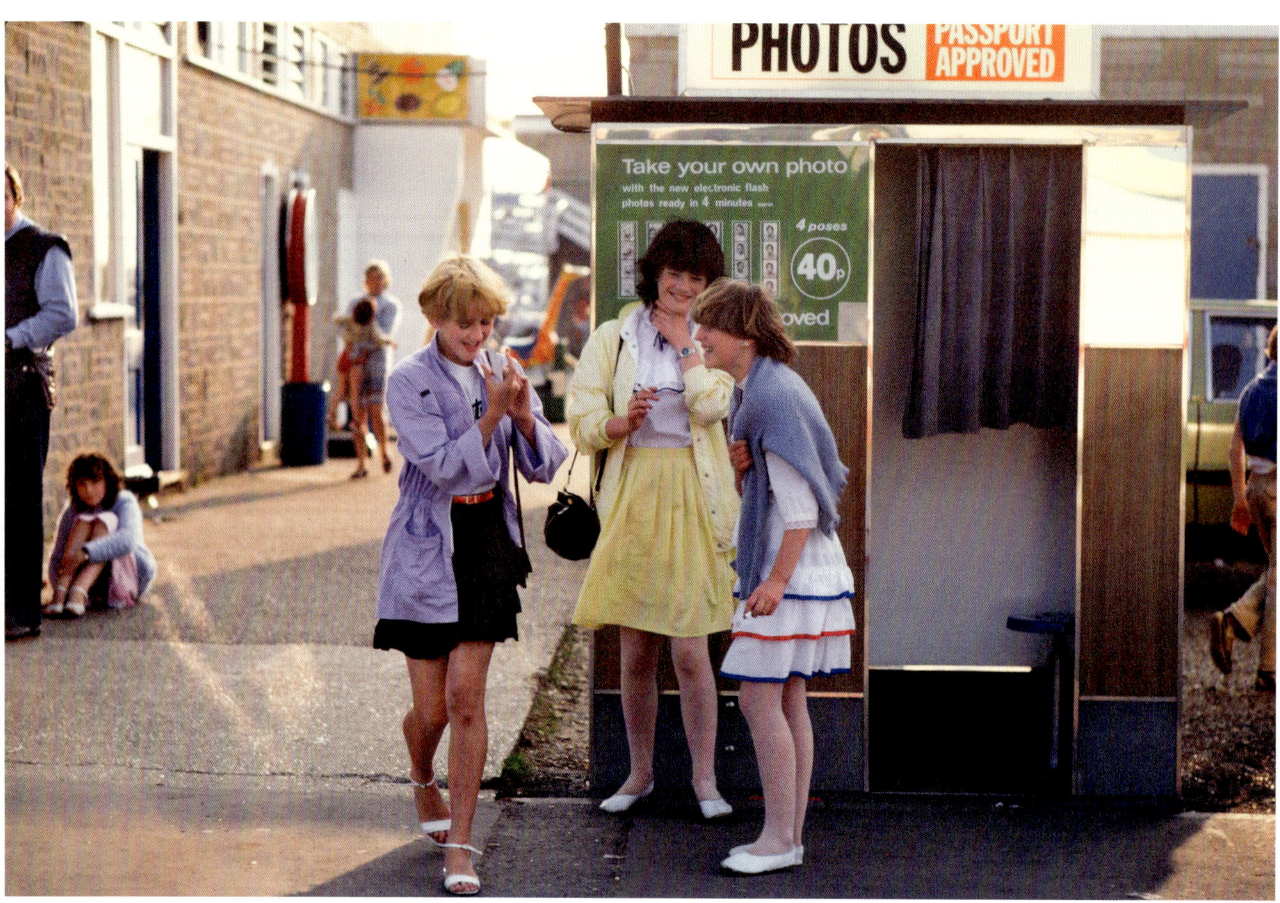
PHOTOS
PASSPORT
APPROVED
Take your own photo
with the new electronic flash
photos ready in 4 minutes
4 poses
40p
oved

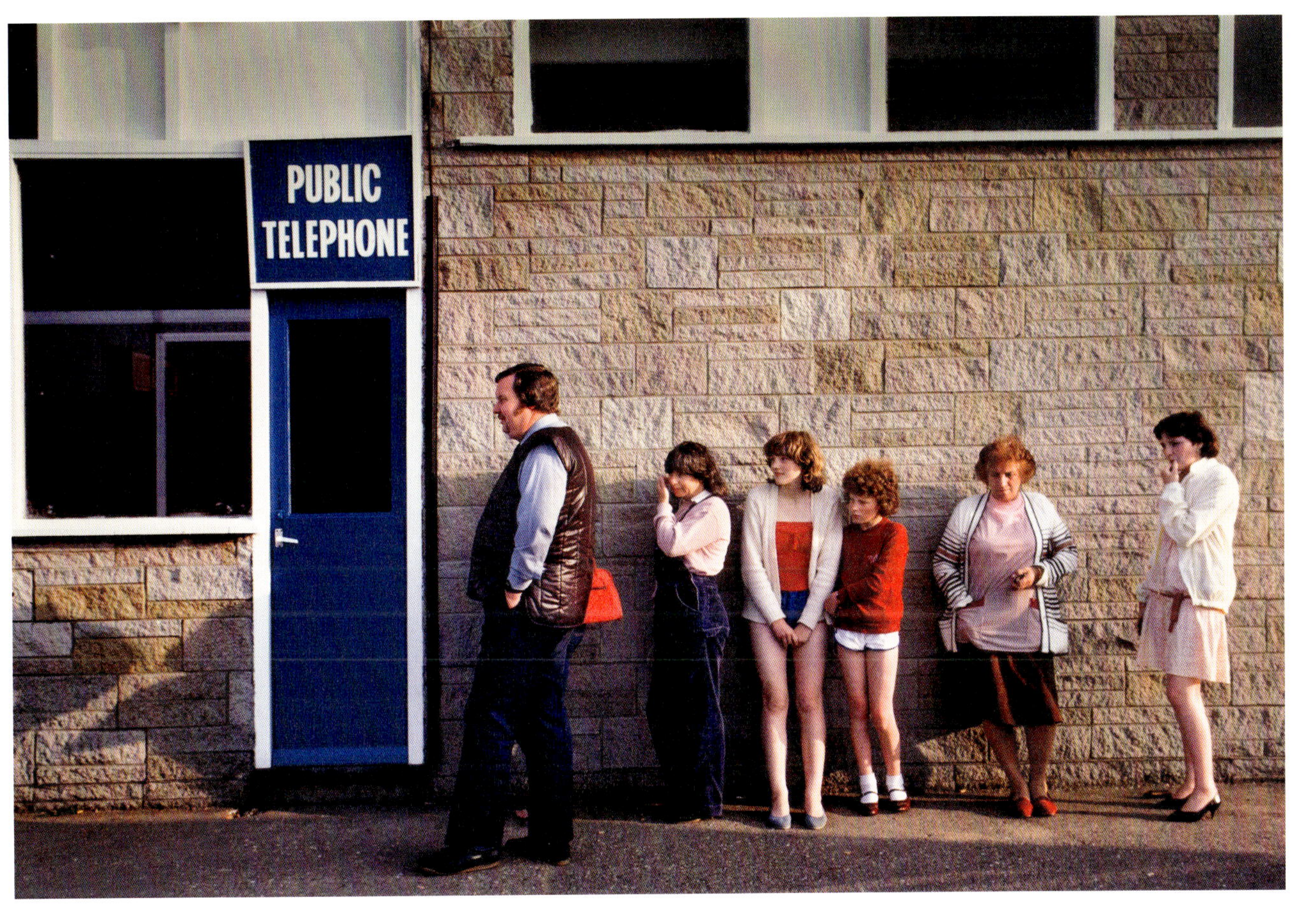

Girls enjoying their portraits from the photo booth
as others queue to make a phone call.

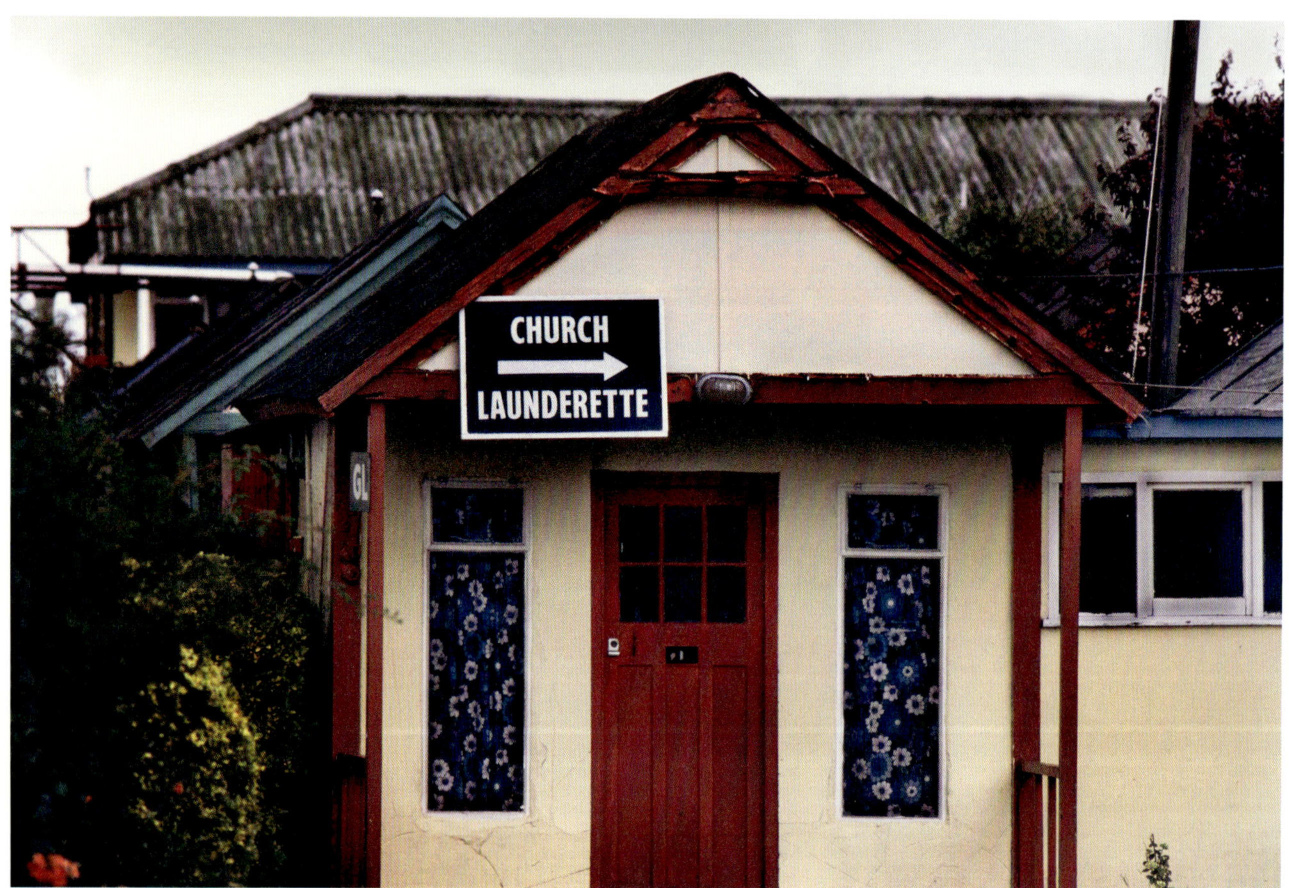

CHURCH
LAUNDERETTE

**Having a lovely time with good fellowship.
The Bible studies are very good. It's good
to be among so many Christians.**

Text written on a found postcard, Butlin's Skegness, 1985

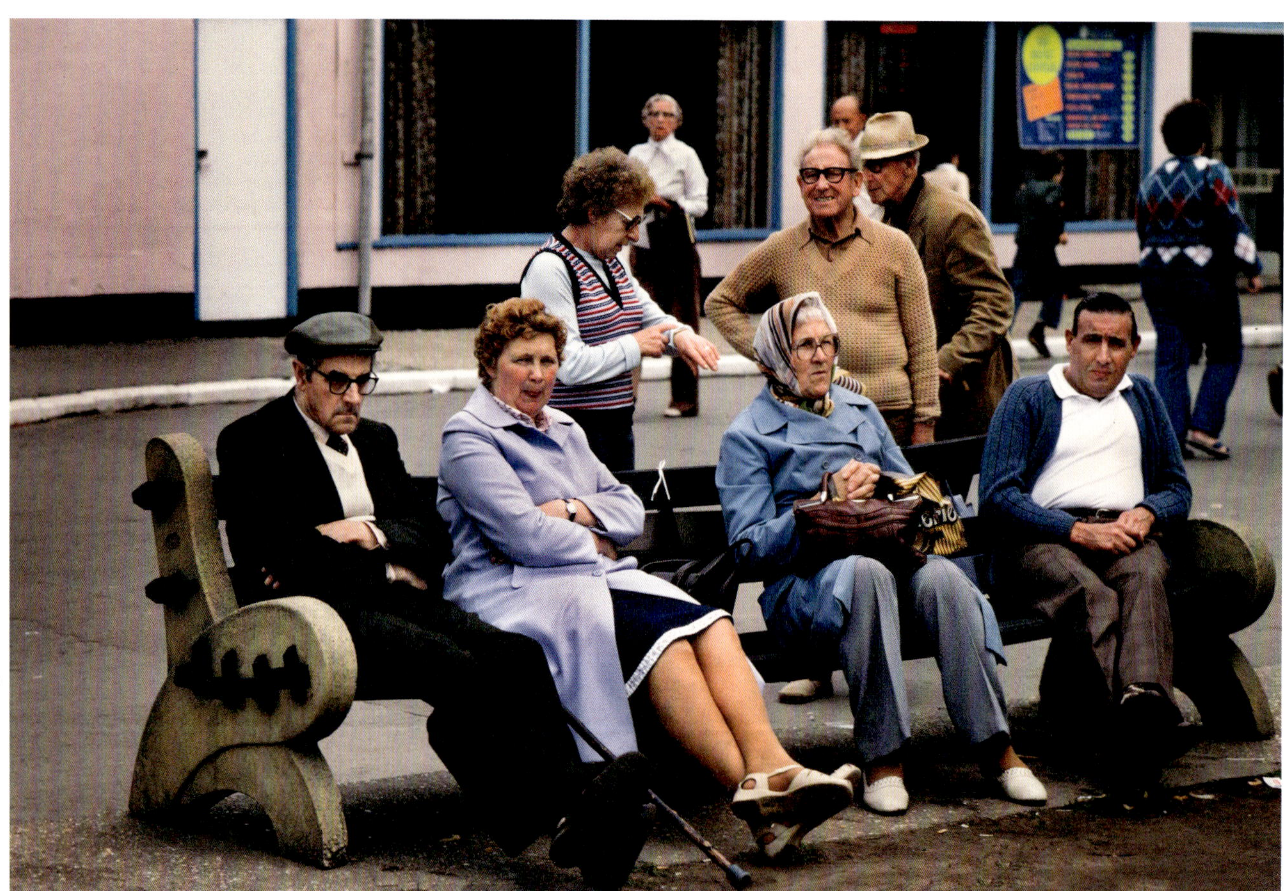

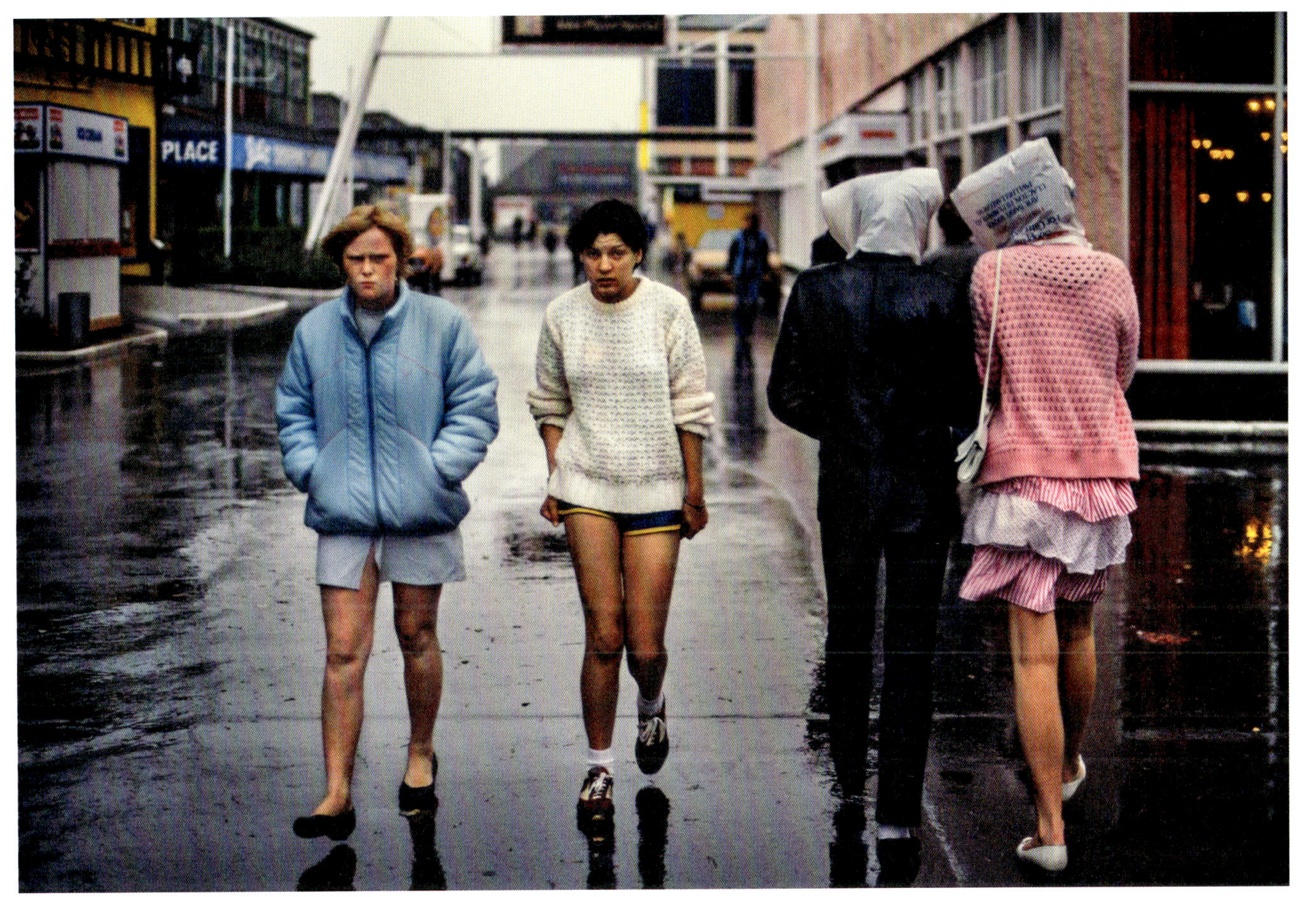

Campers dealing with the Lincolnshire wind and rain.

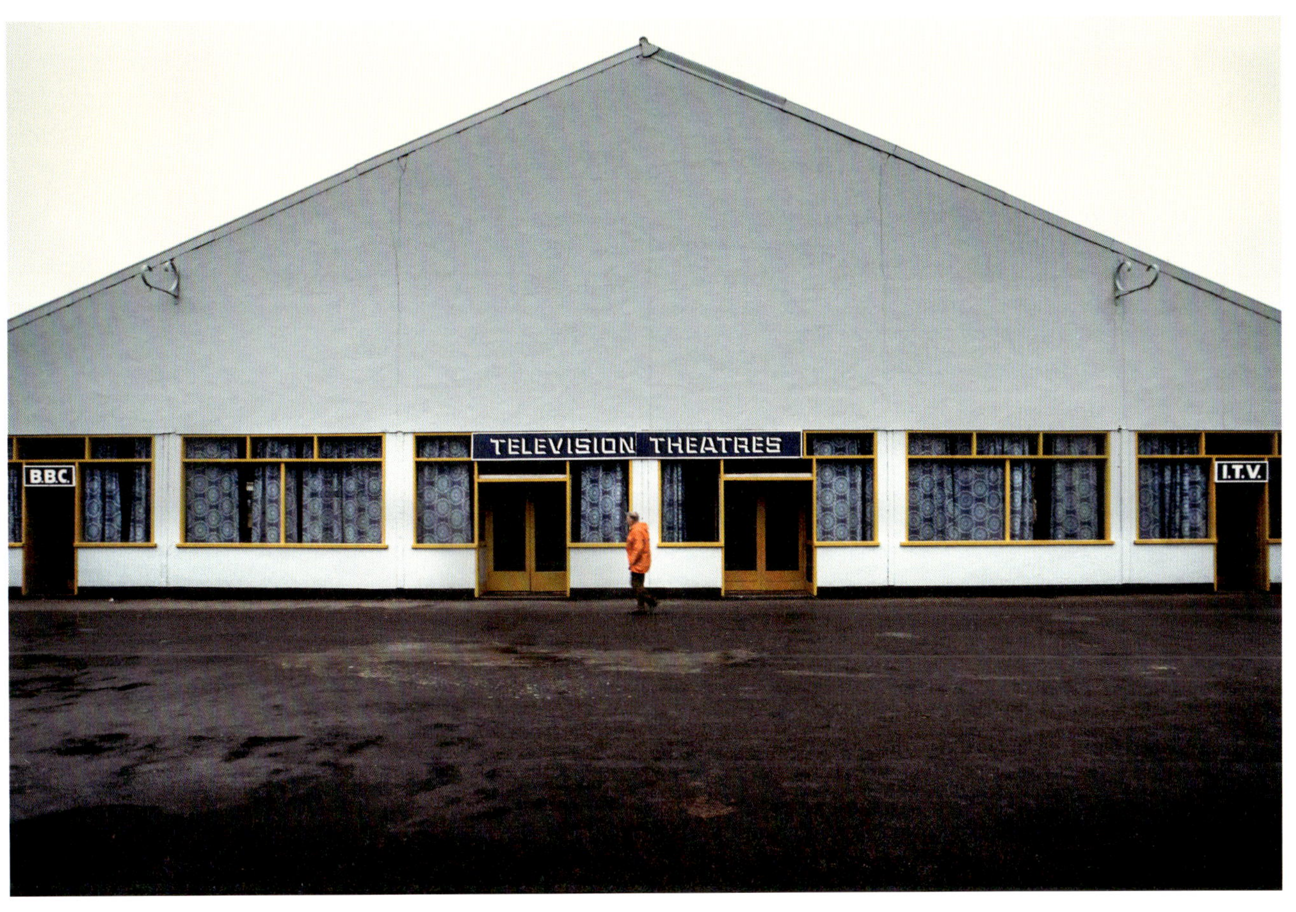

The guest chalets were not equipped with TVs in 1982. Television theatres showed only two channels in rooms 30 metres apart.

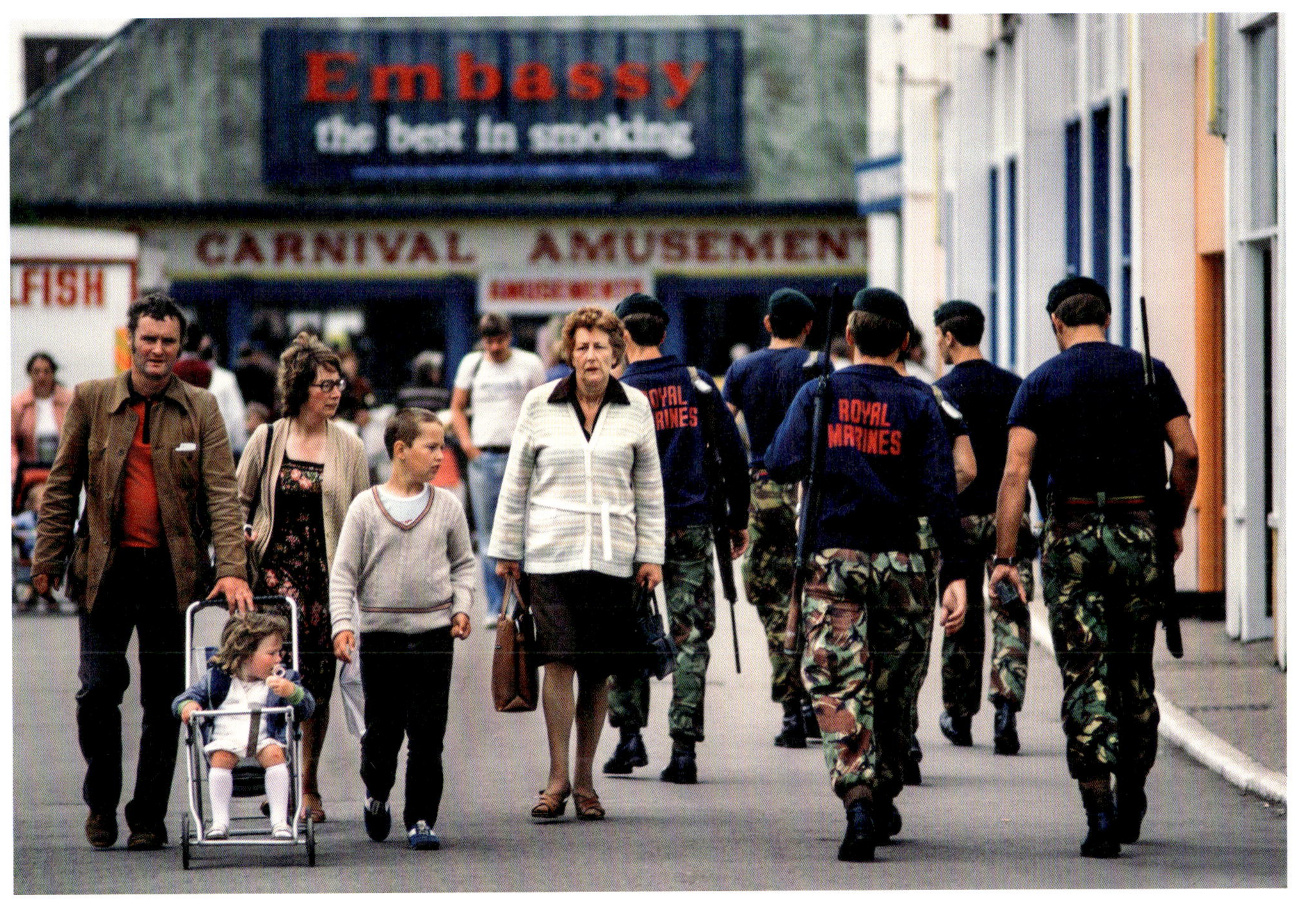

A team of Marines visiting the camp to promote
the Army during the 1982 Falklands War.

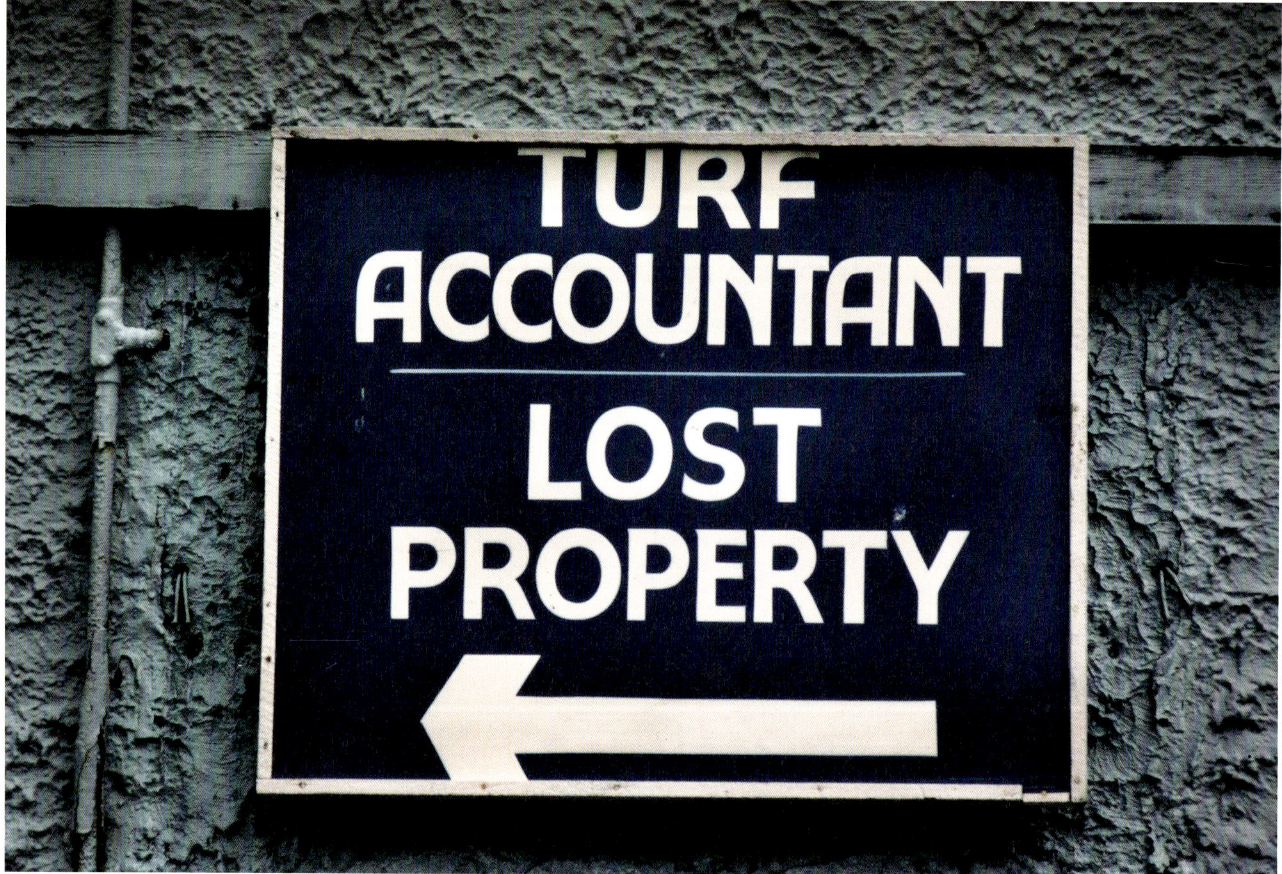

TURF
ACCOUNTANT
LOST
PROPERTY

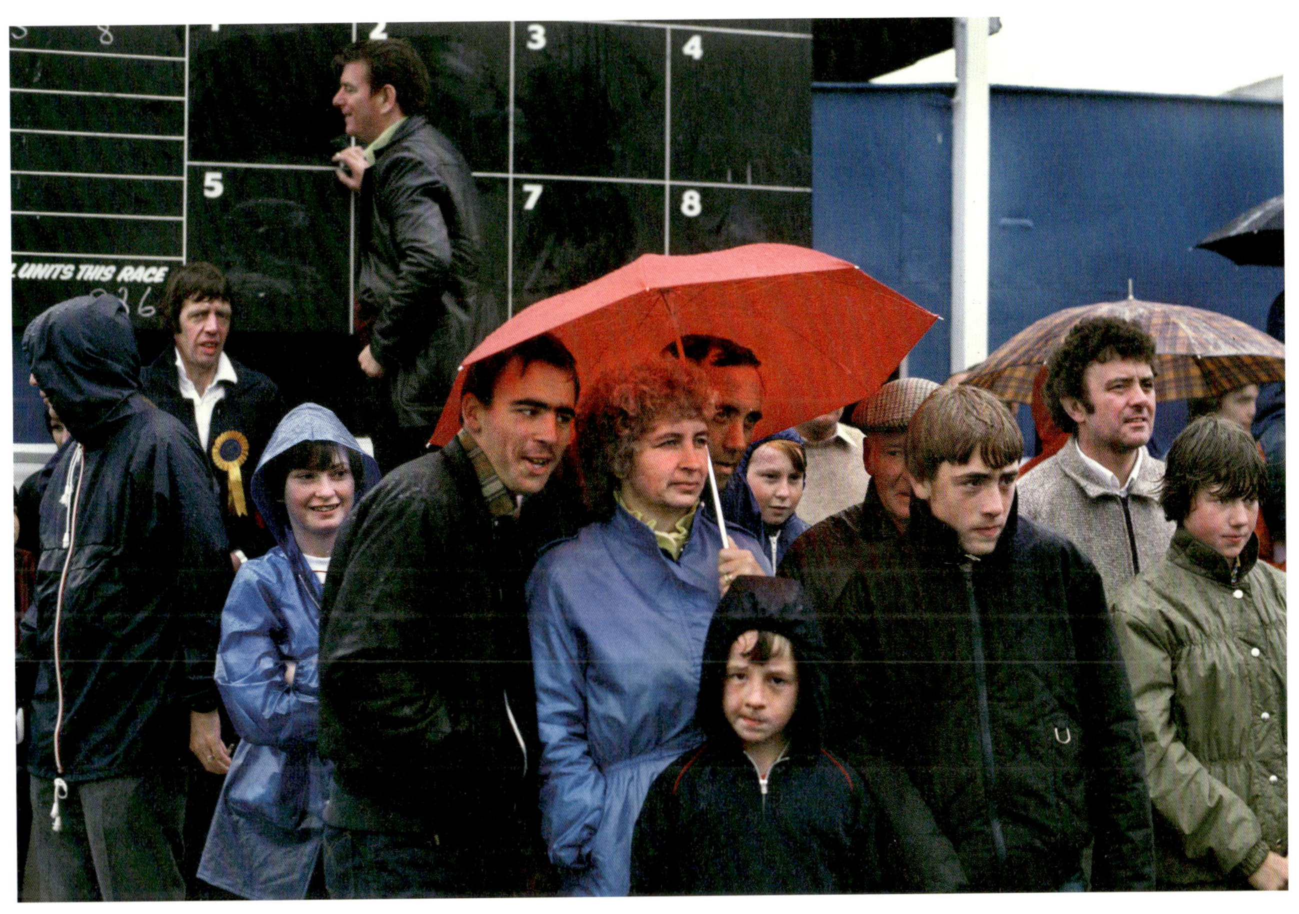

A sign points towards lost property and the bookies (turf accountant),
while punters watch the camp's donkey derby.

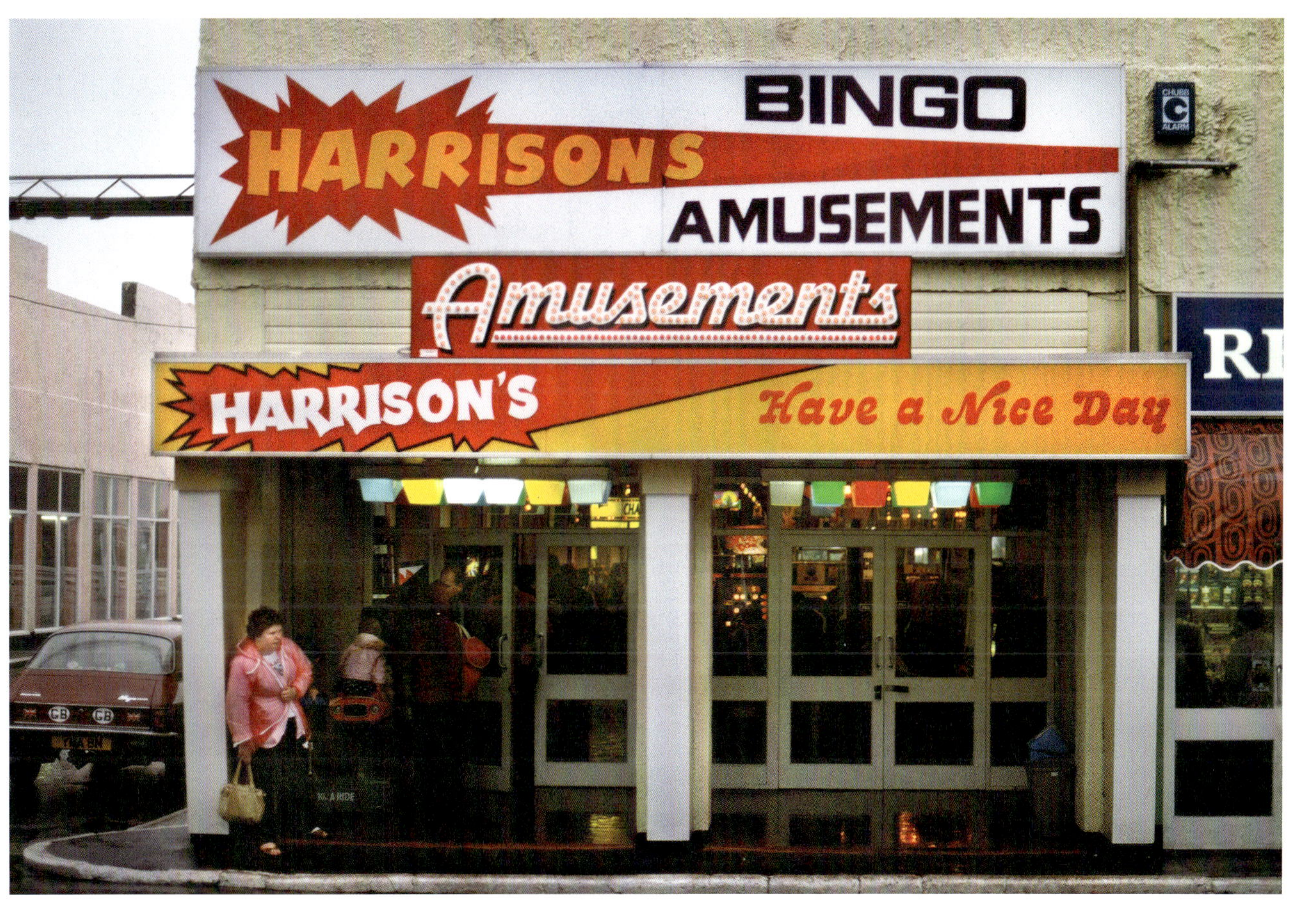

The amusement arcade provided good shelter and
entertainment when the wet weather struck.

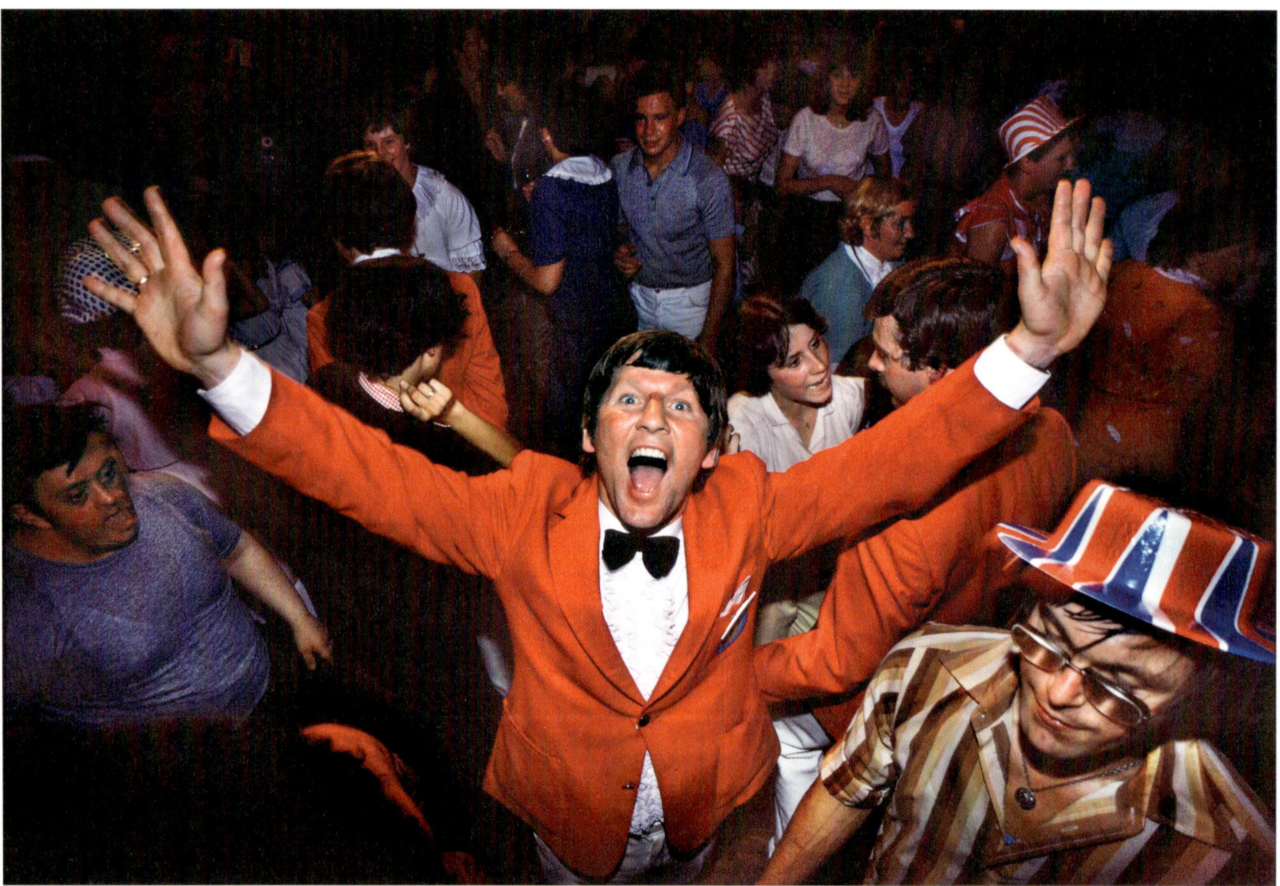

A Redcoat is a guide, philosopher and friend
to many thousands of holidaymakers

A Redcoat is a good mixer, is patient
and tolerant with all kinds of people

A Redcoat works a hard and tiring day,
their ready smile is just as genuine
last thing at night as it was at breakfast time

Advice sheet given to Redcoat applicants, c.1960s

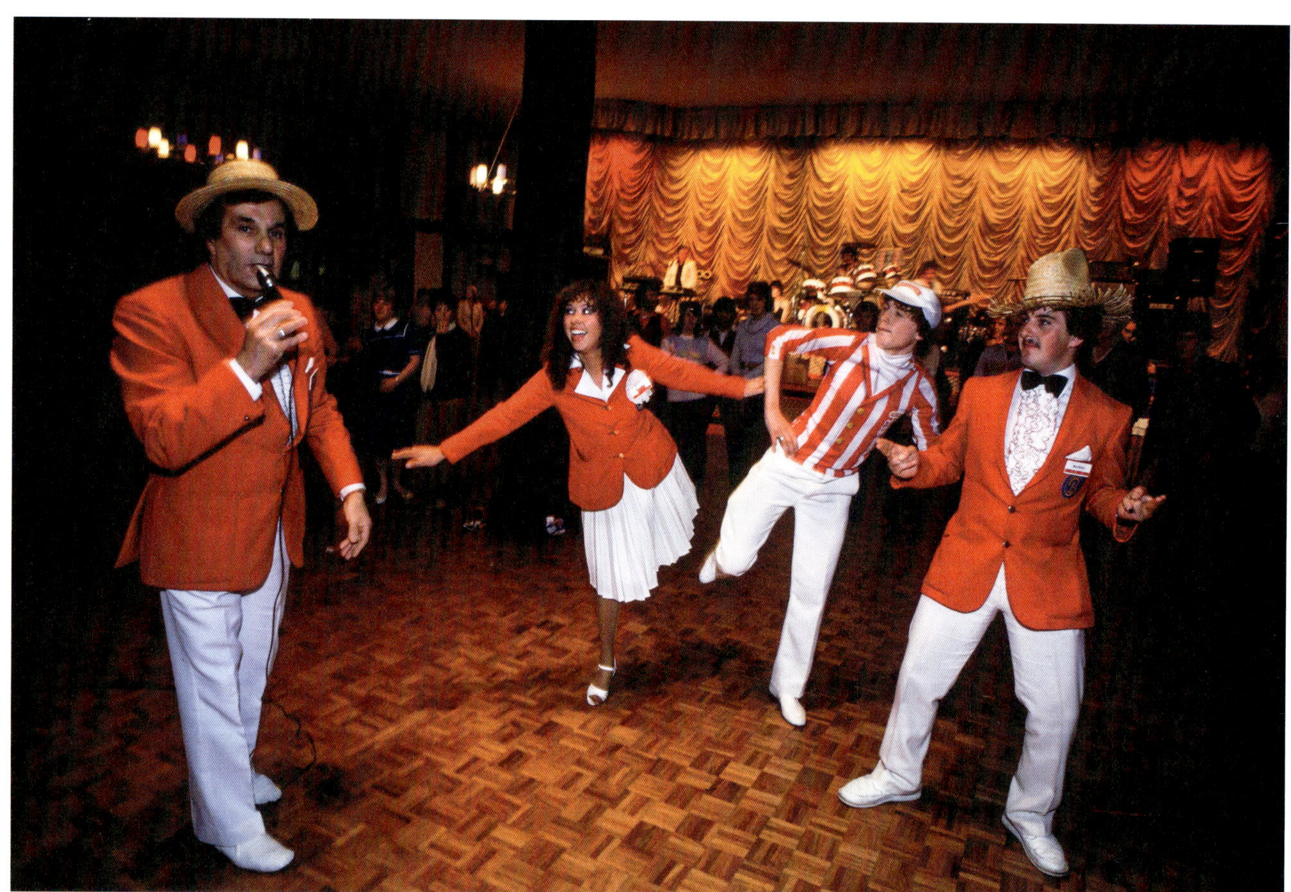

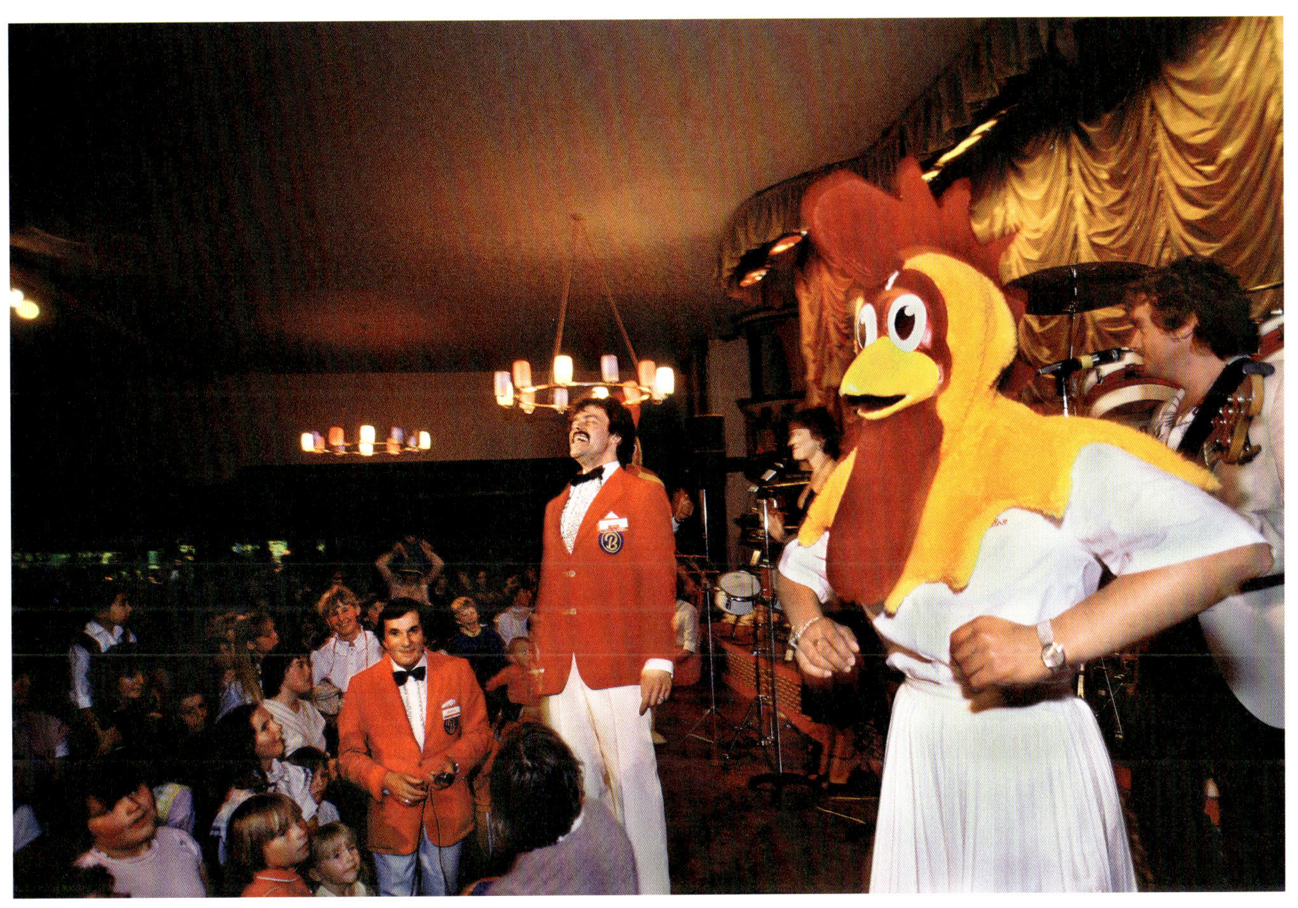

The Rooster Rock, a novelty dance sponsored by
Paxo stuffing, taking place in the Empress Ballroom.

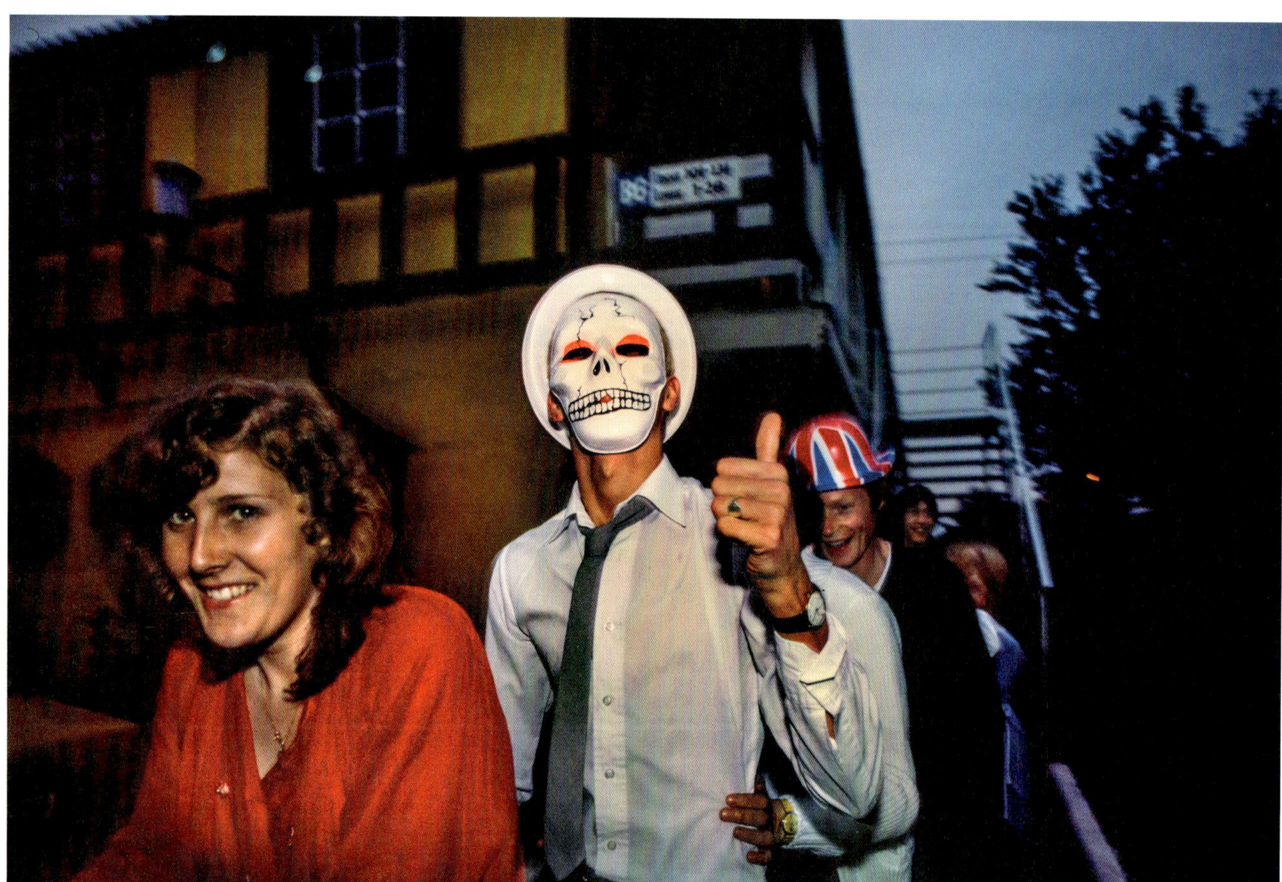

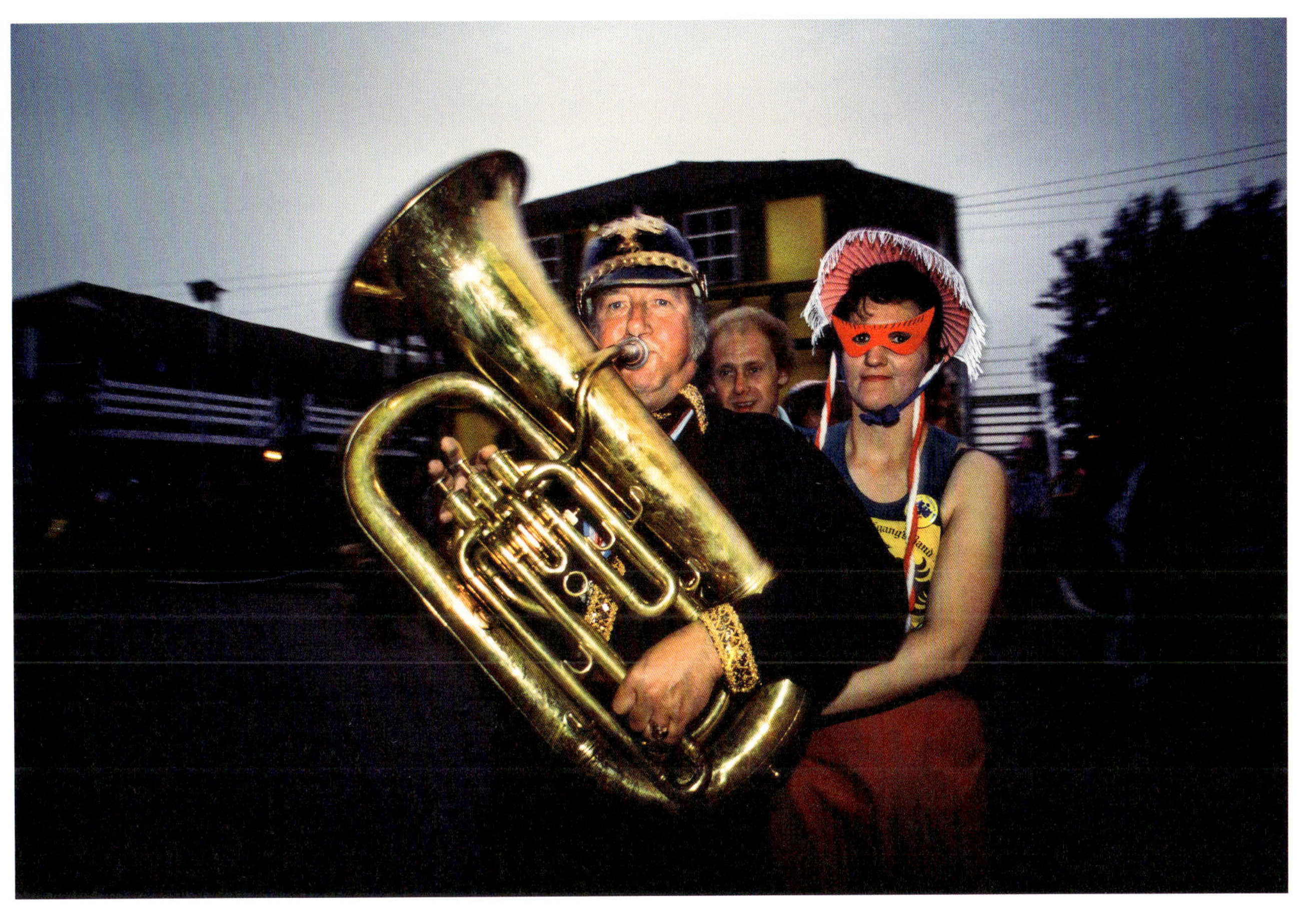

Resident performer Baron Wolfgang with his tuba, leading
a conga through the camp from the Bier Keller pub.

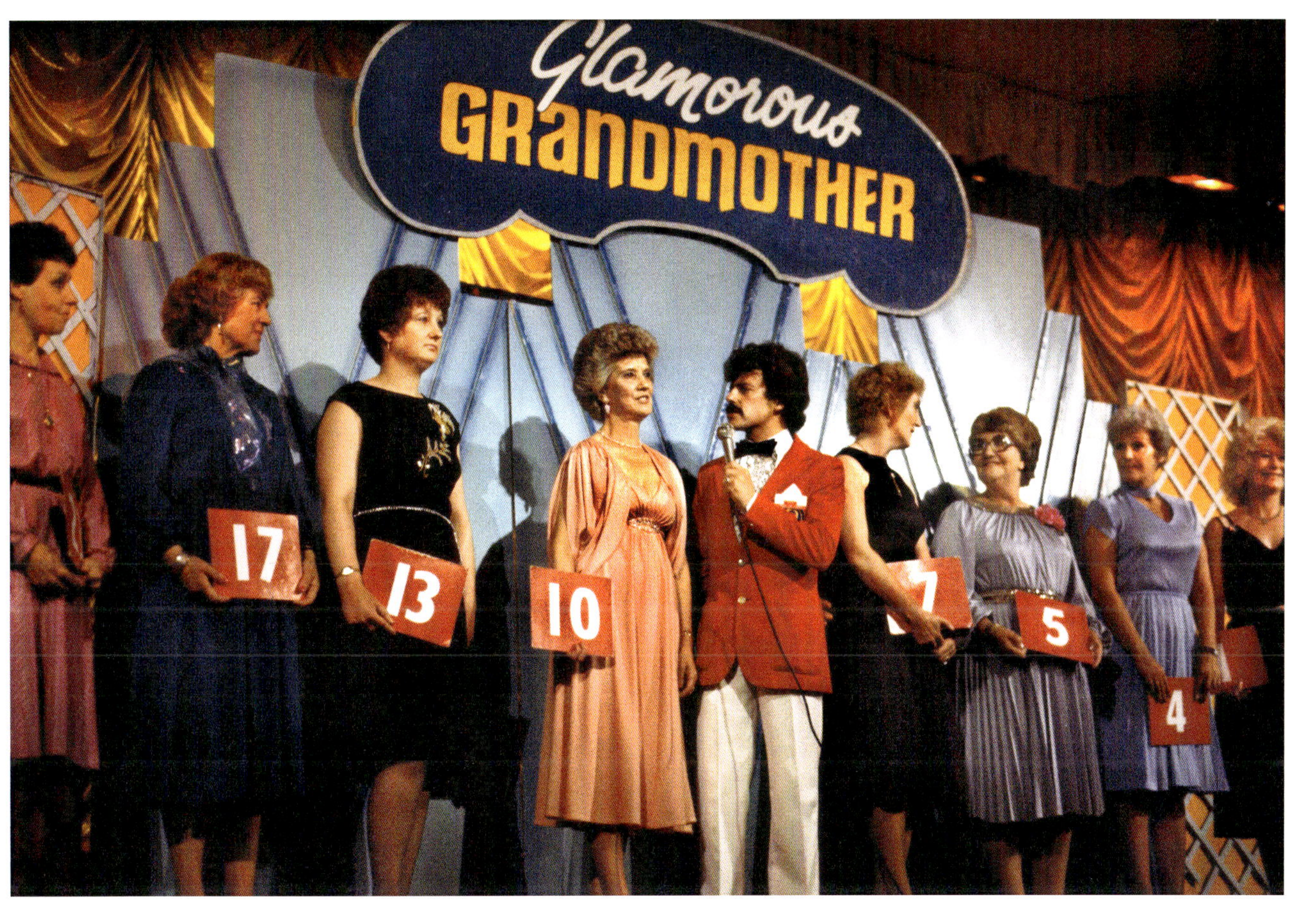

The final of the weekly Glamorous Grandmother competition,
which was introduced in 1955 and continued to run until 1995.

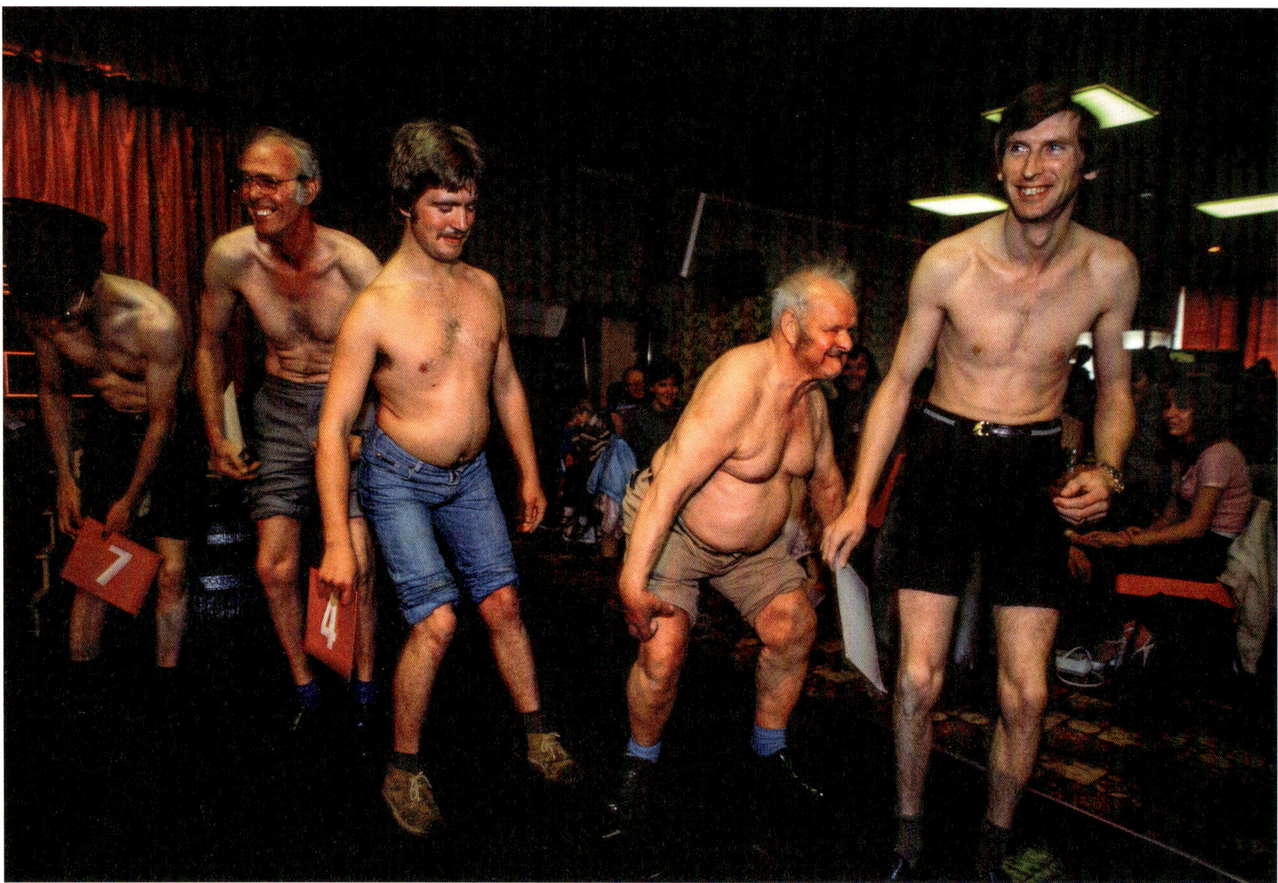

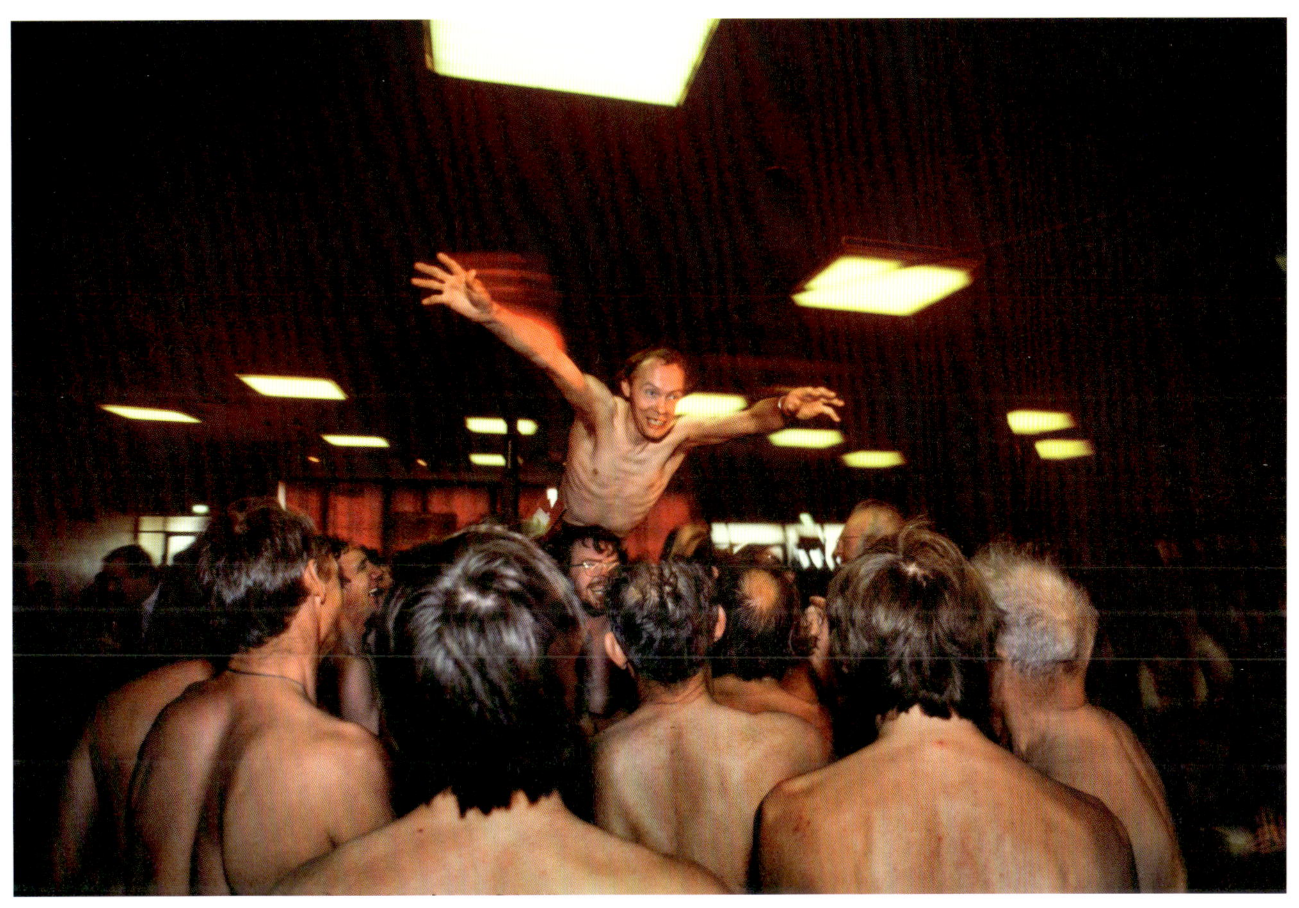

The Most Knobbly Knees competition, with the
winner crowd-surfing over his opponents.

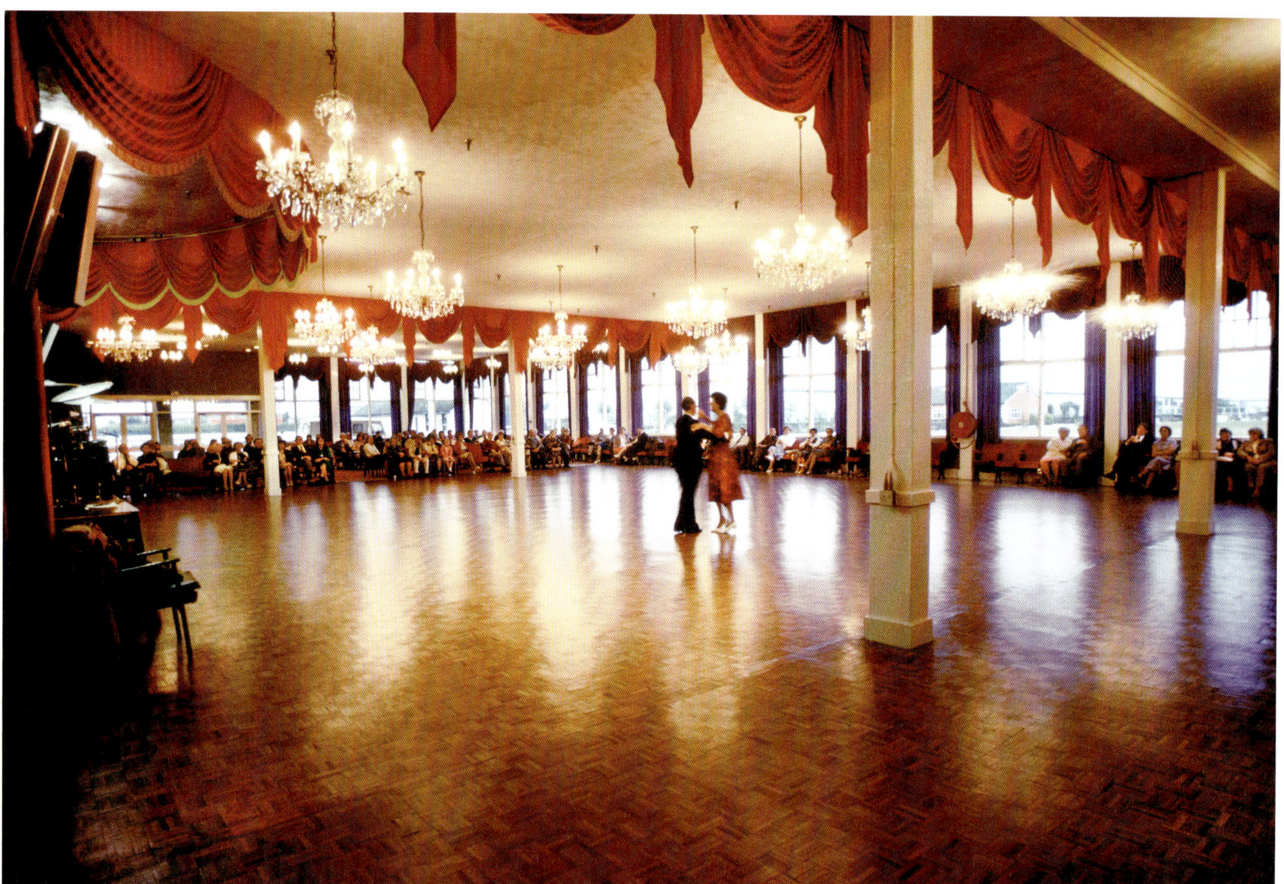

At a holiday camp I found a lovely romance
At a holiday camp one summer's day
Her tiny chalet was just next door but two
When she said: 'Hello' then my heart said:
'Oh, here's the girl for you.'

Extract from the song 'At a Holiday Camp'

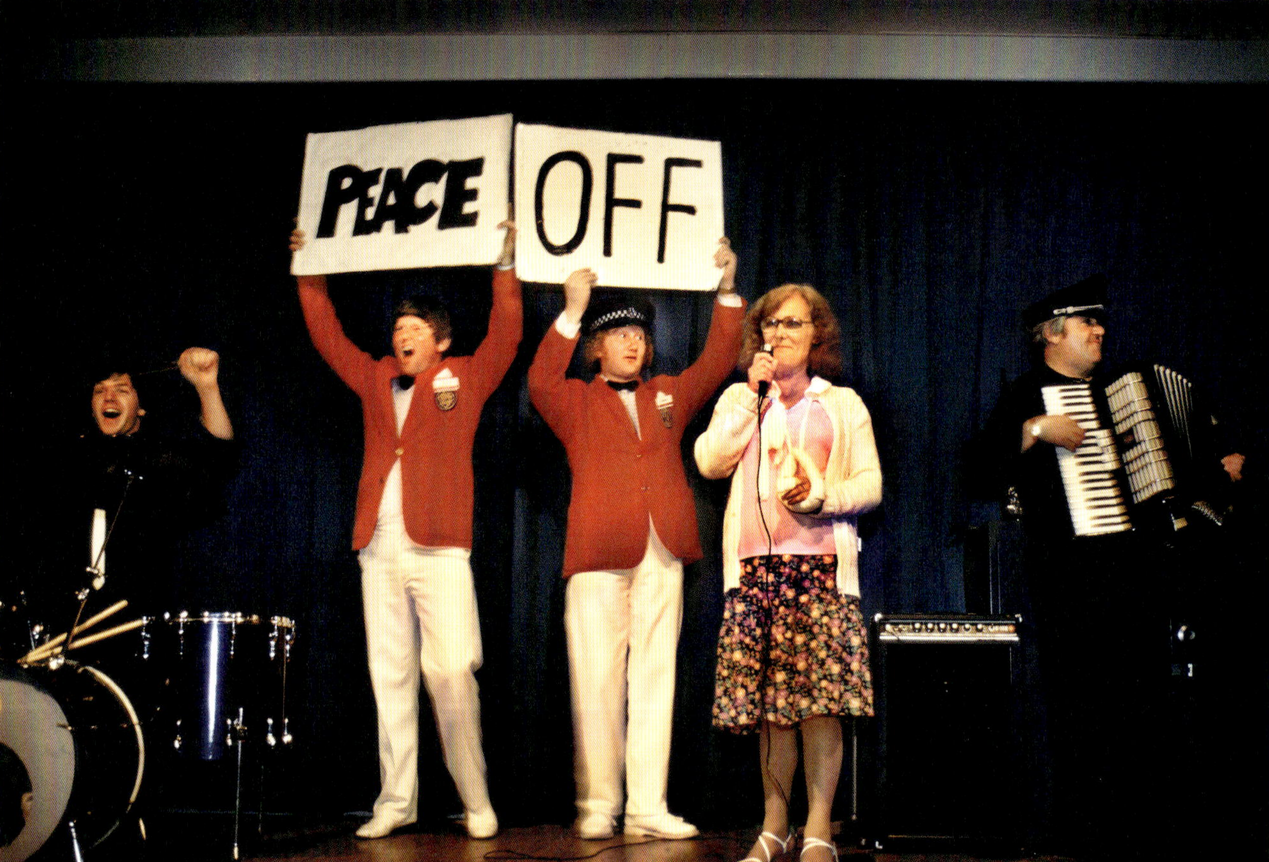

PEACE
OFF

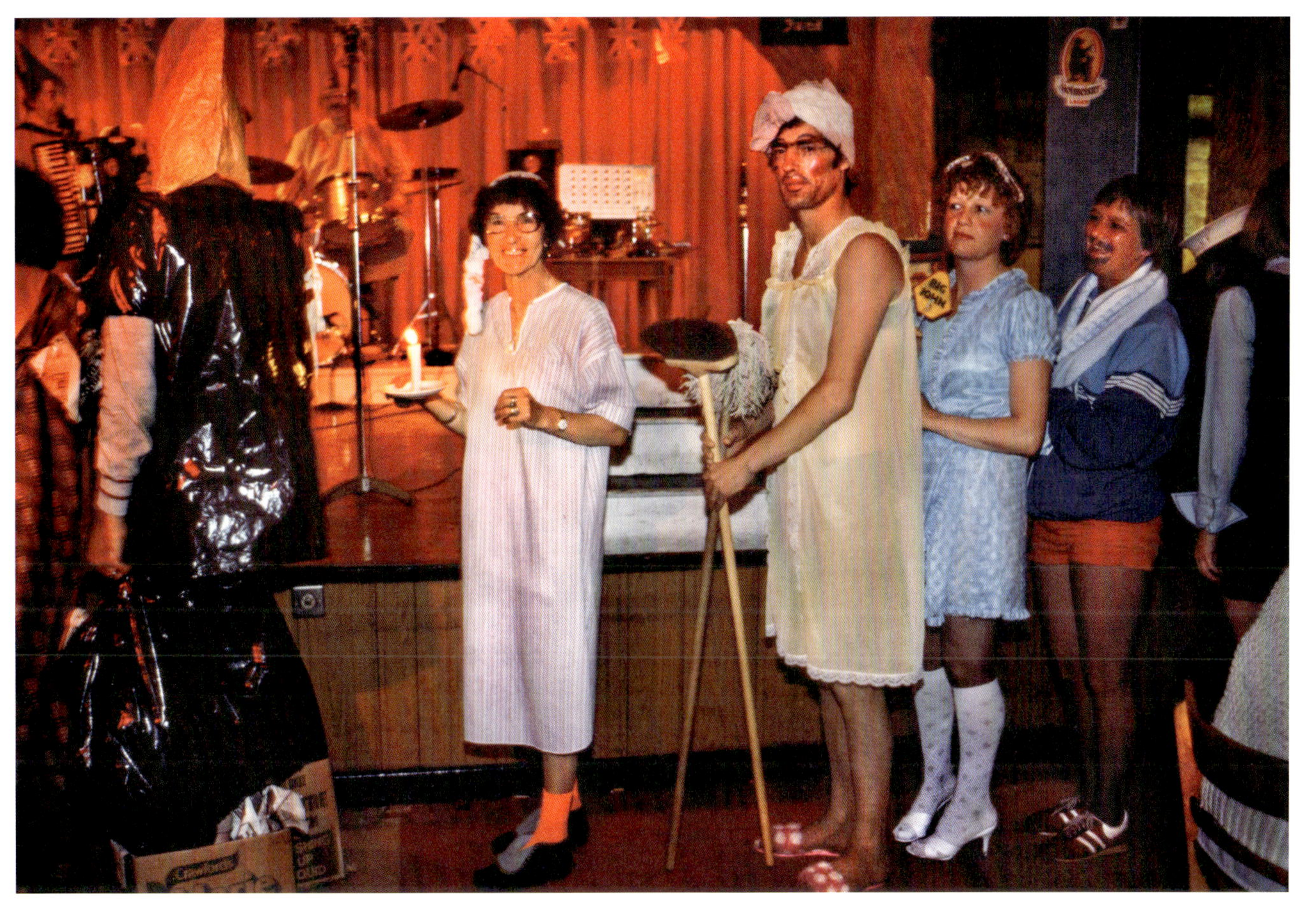

Campers were invited to take part in talent contests and fancy dress competitions as part of the evening entertainment.

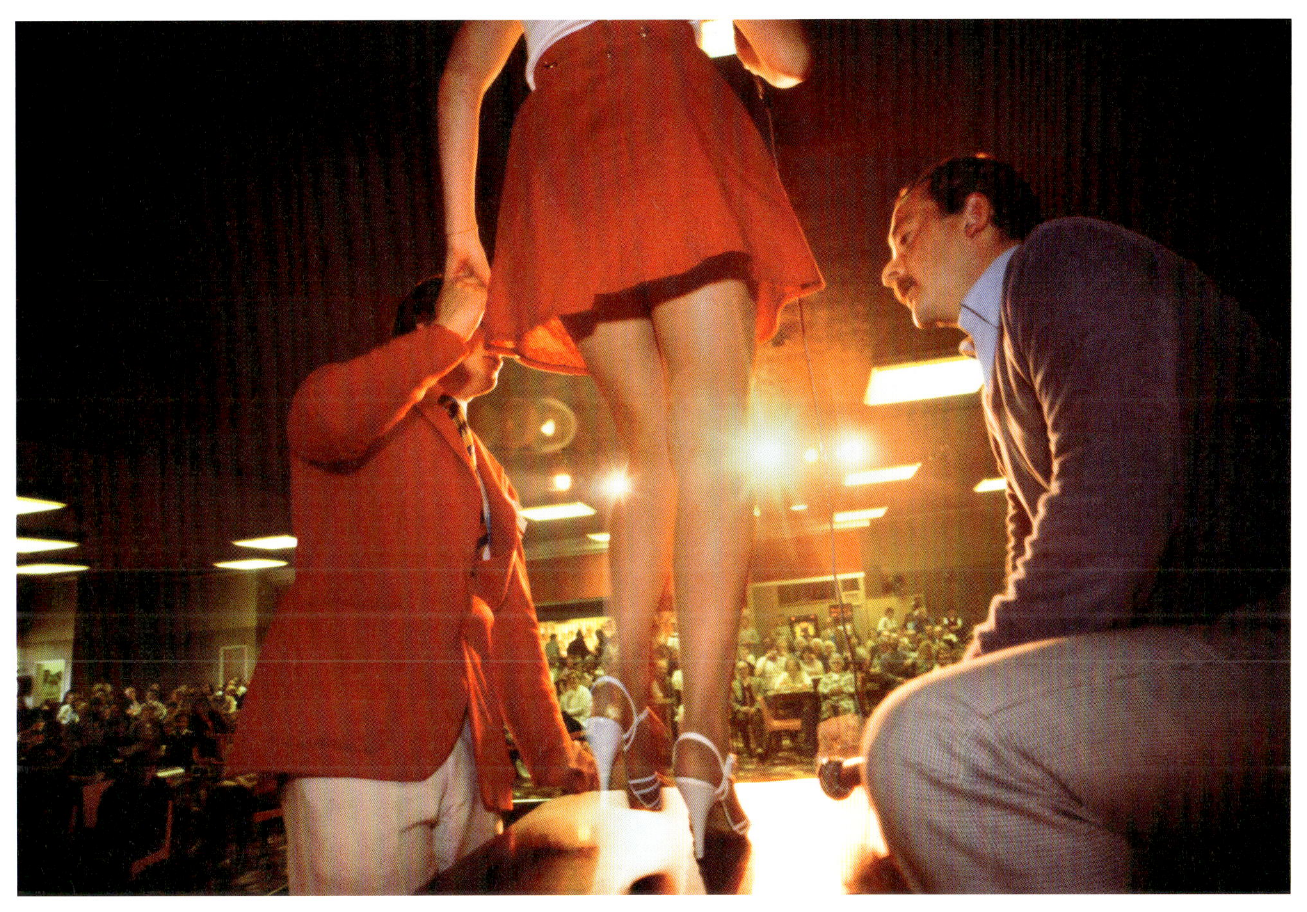

Two men closely judging the Miss Lovely Legs
of Great Britain competition.

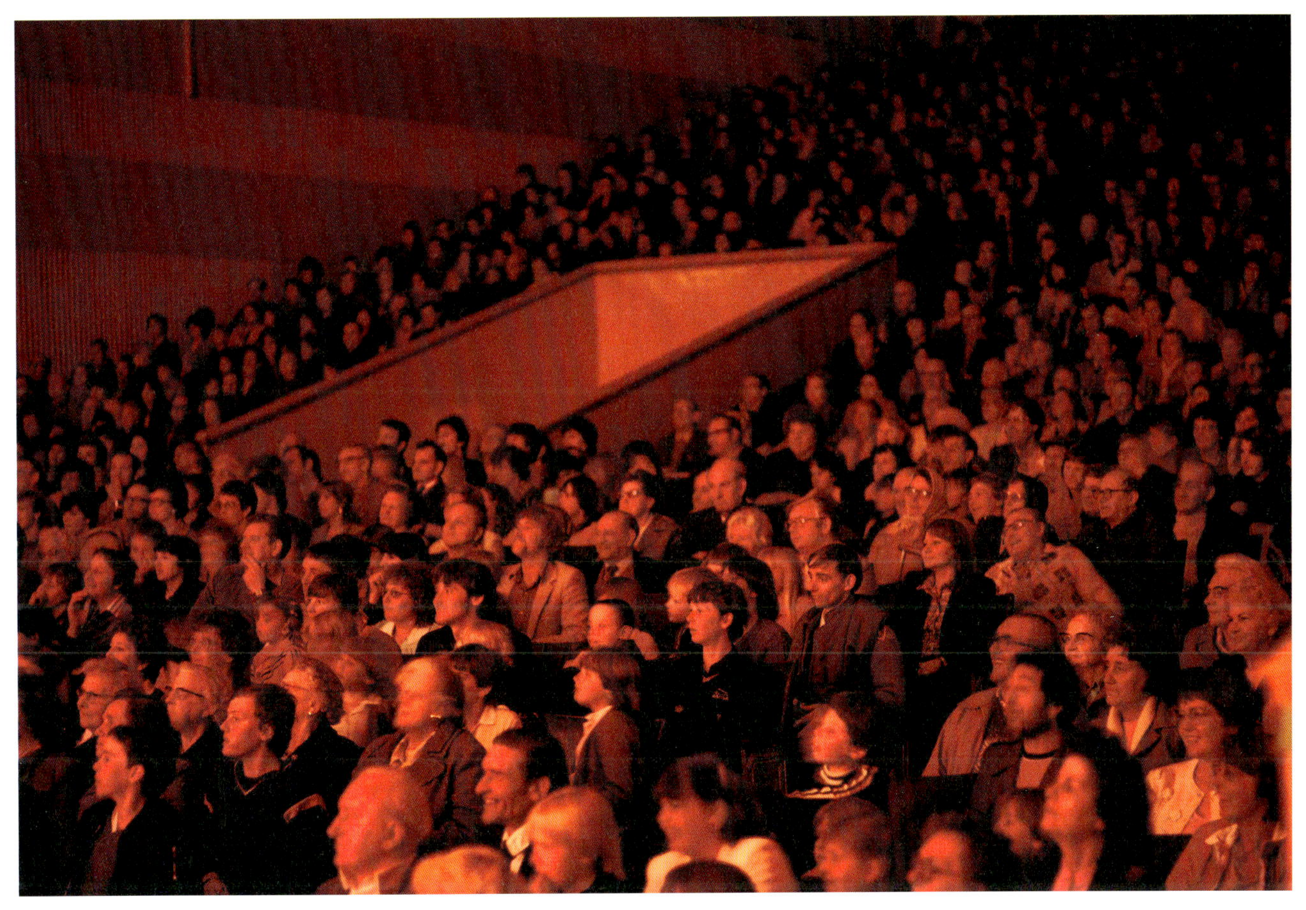

A full house watching the Friday evening
Redcoats Show in the Gaiety Theatre.

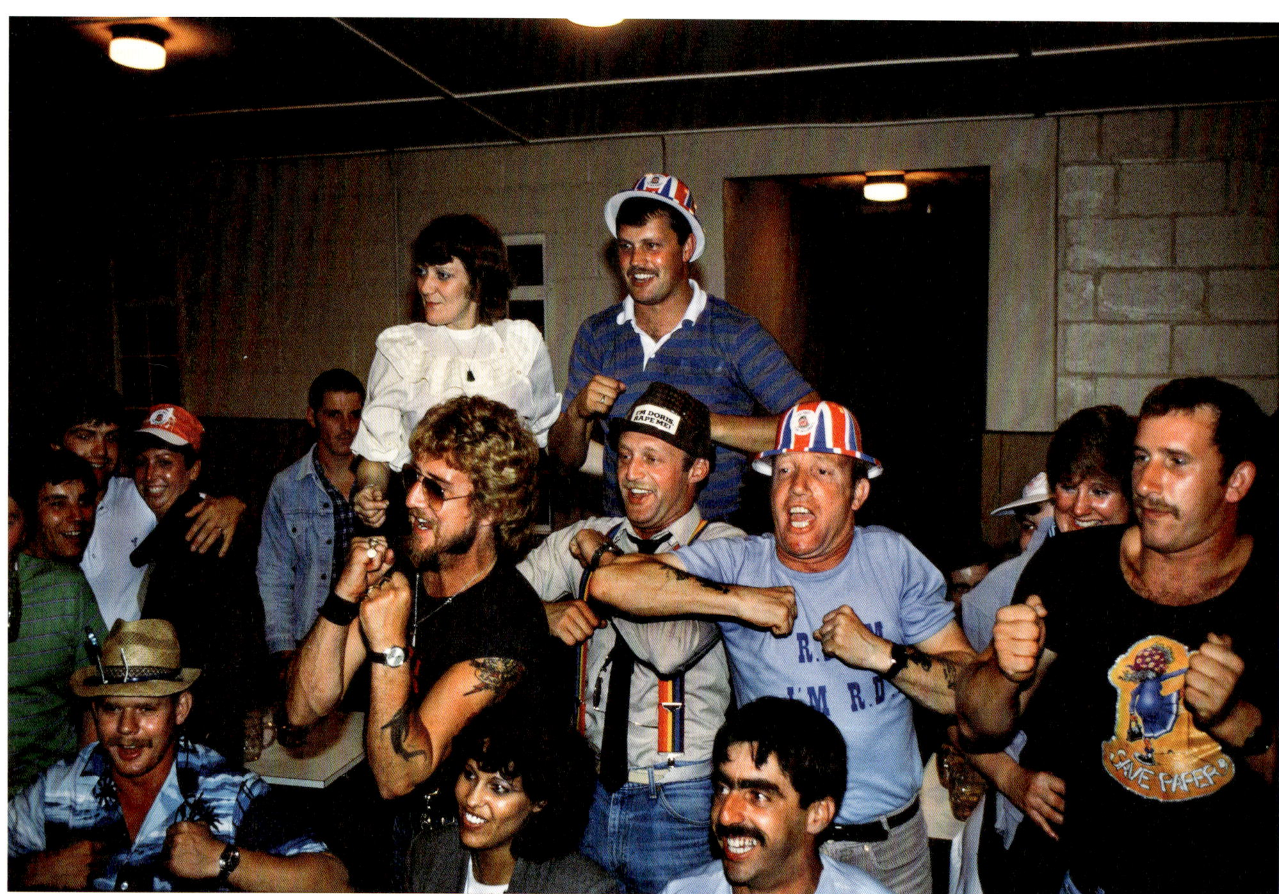

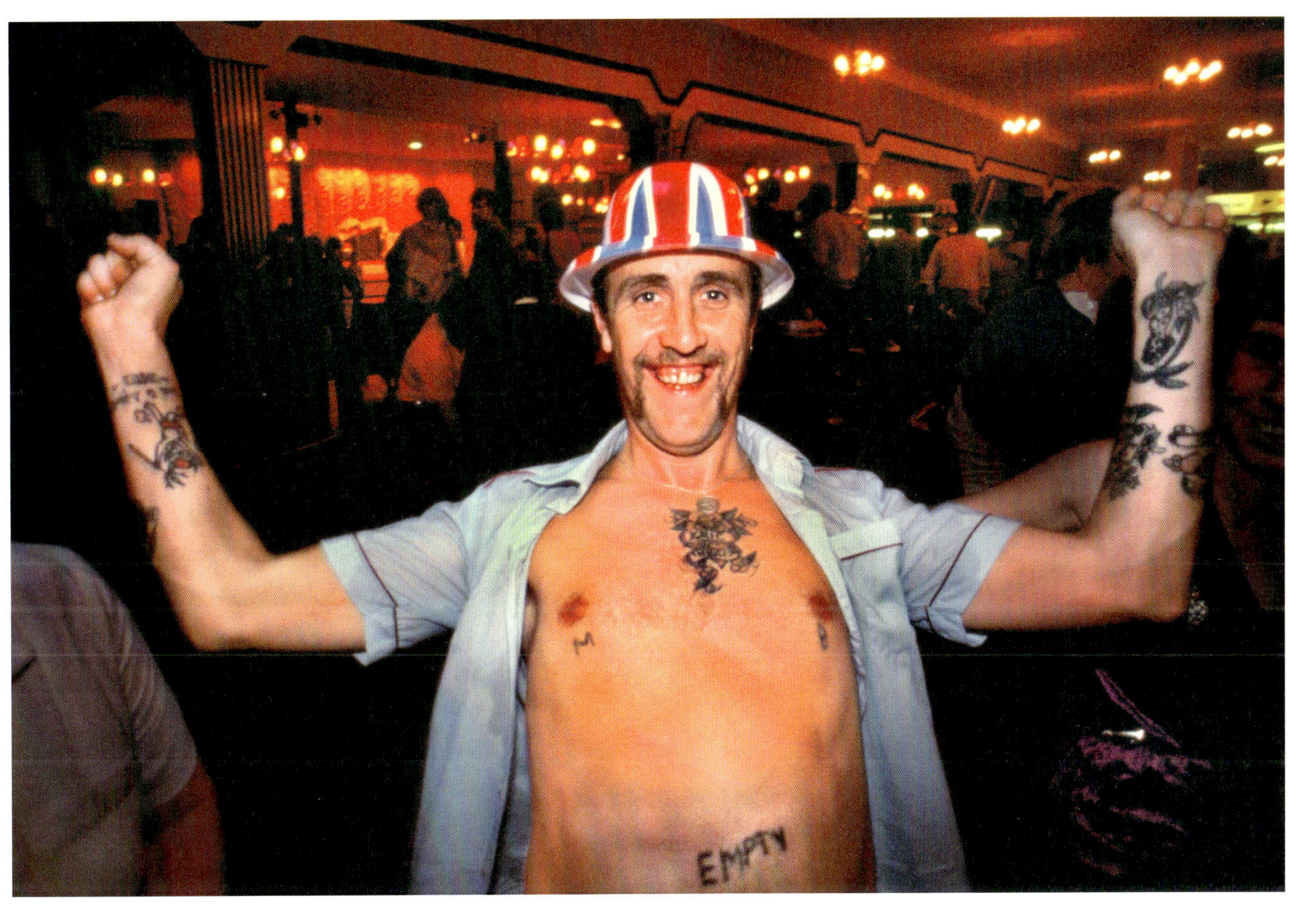

Friday night was carnival night, with the bar staying open longer
to celebrate the end of the holiday week.

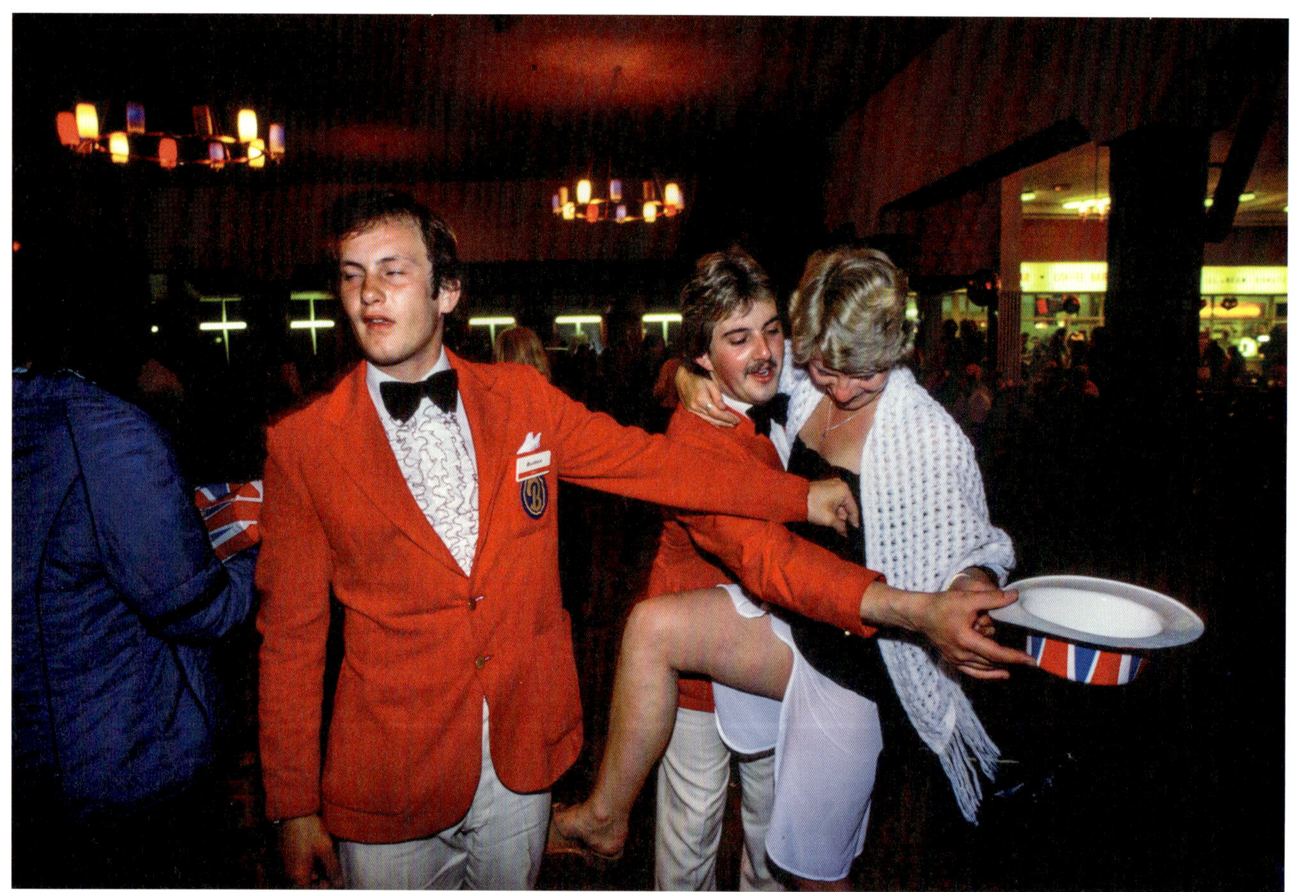

**If you like a bit of this
and quite a lot of that…**

Butlin's advertising slogan, c.1980s

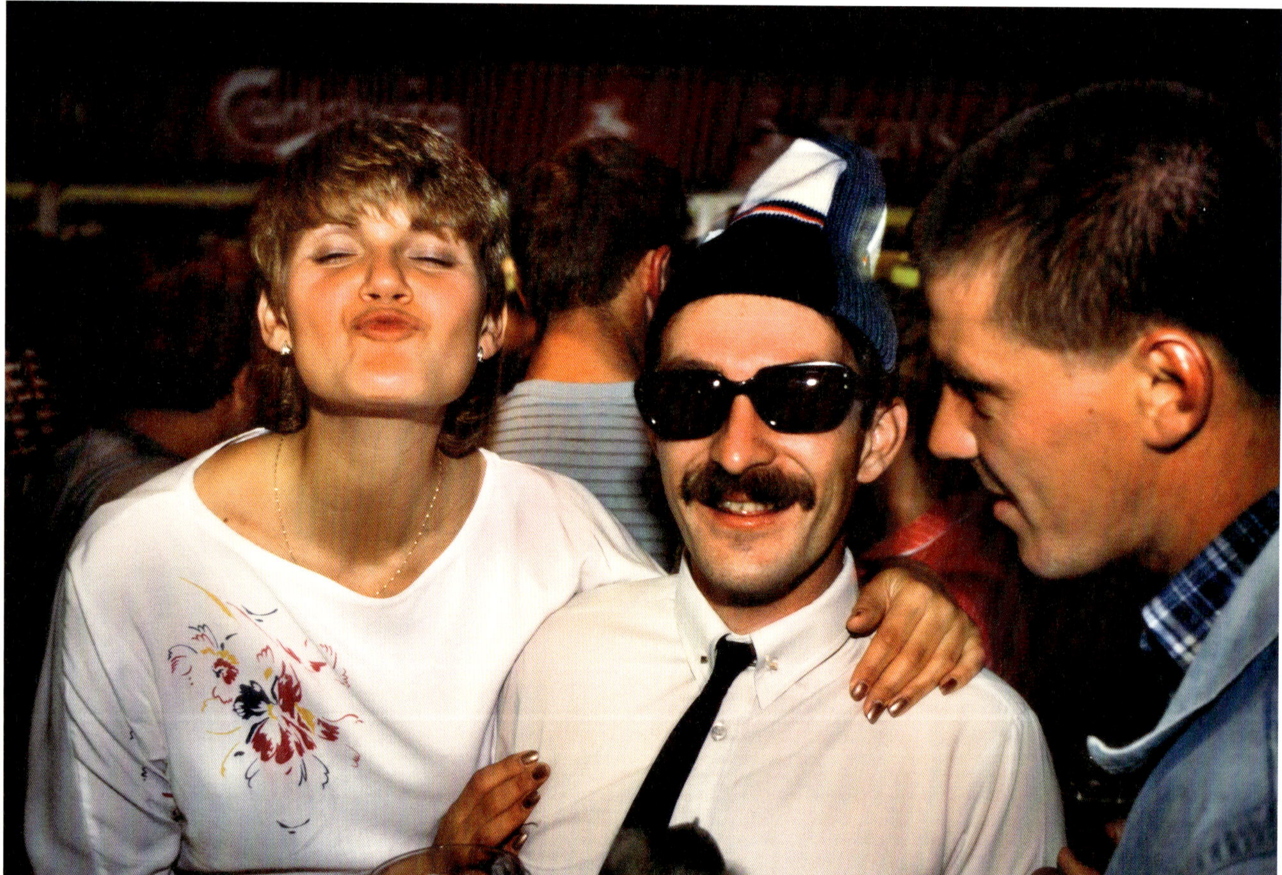

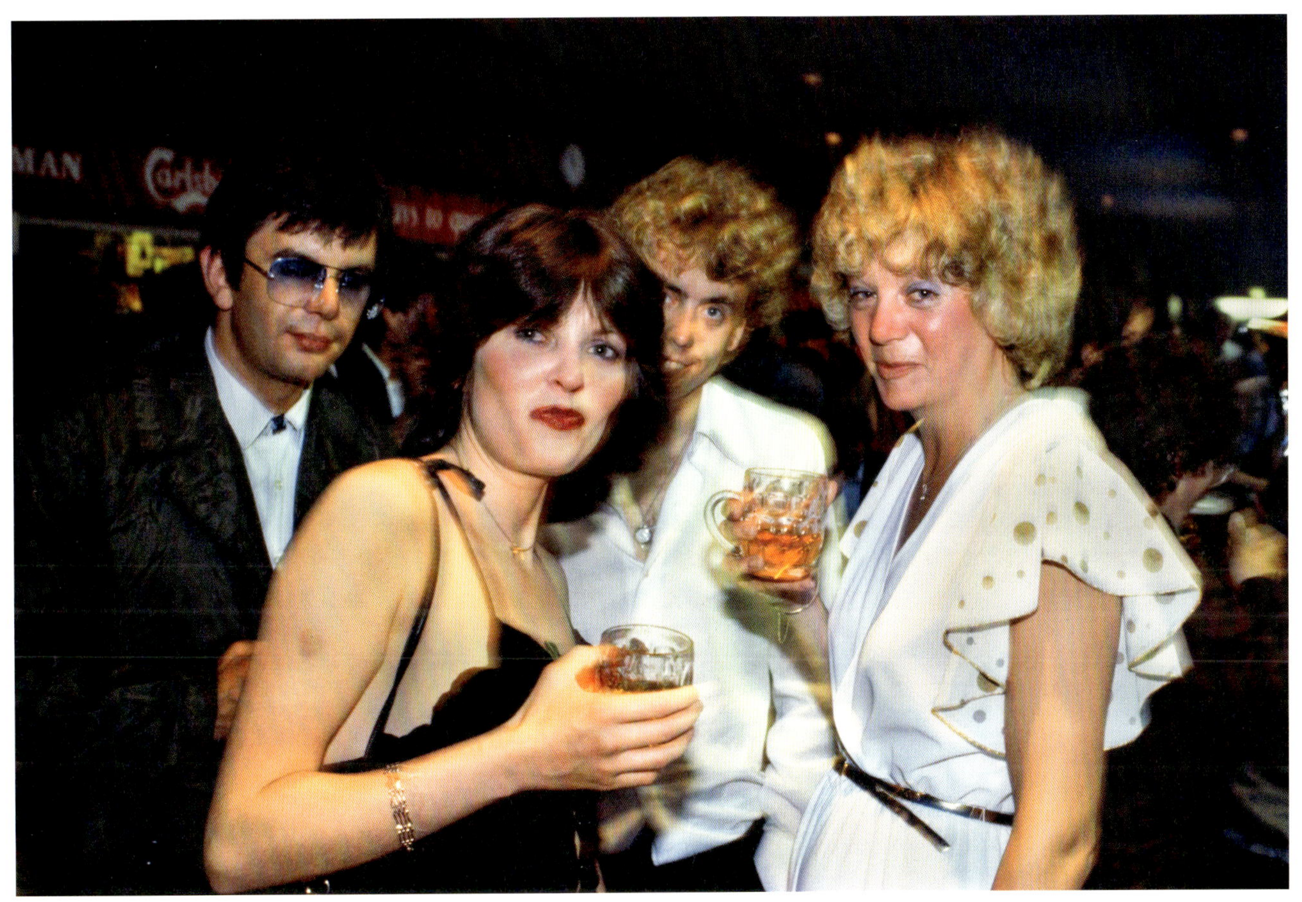

Last orders in the Empress Bar at 12:30pm.

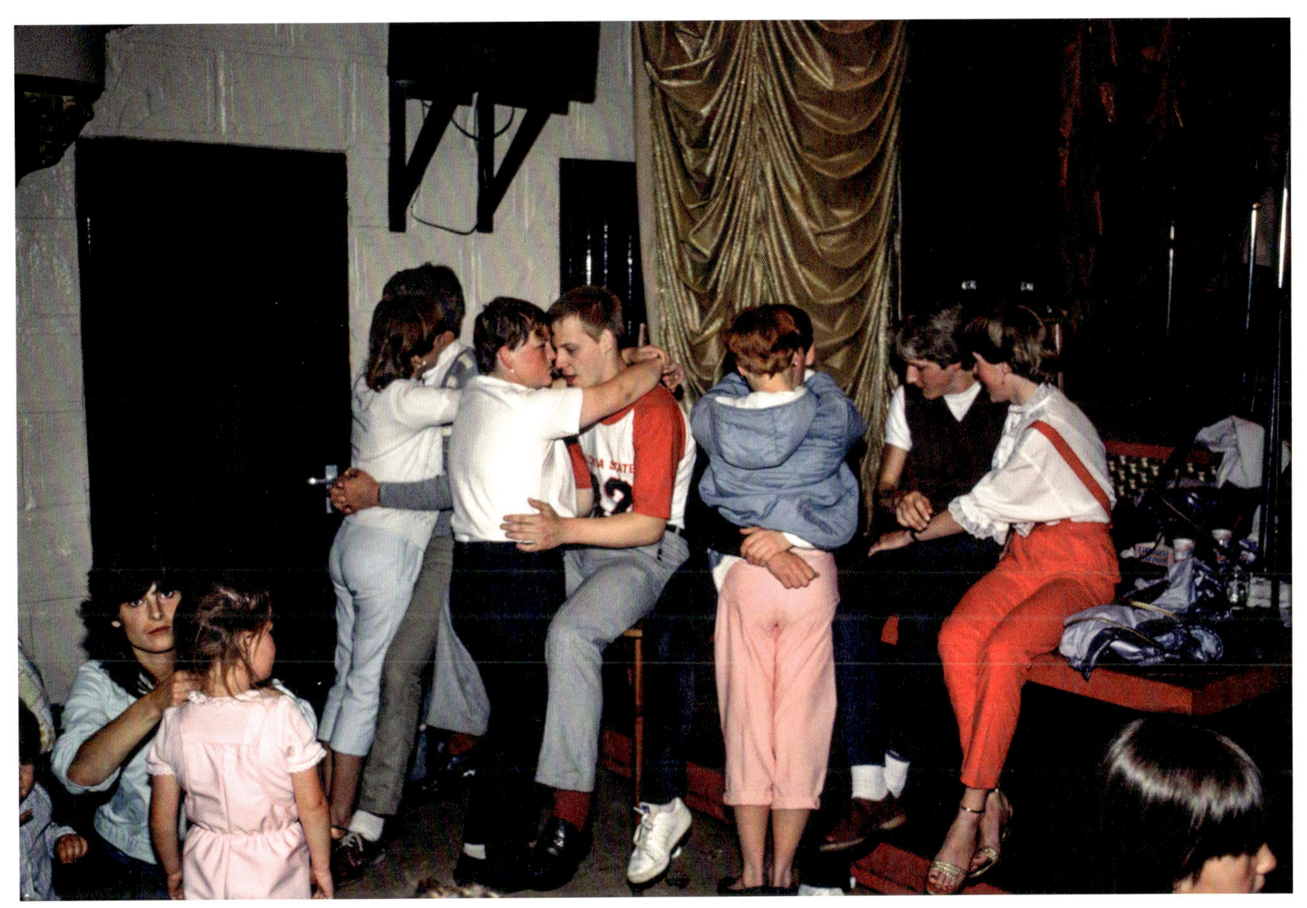

Teenage romance on the last night of the holiday.

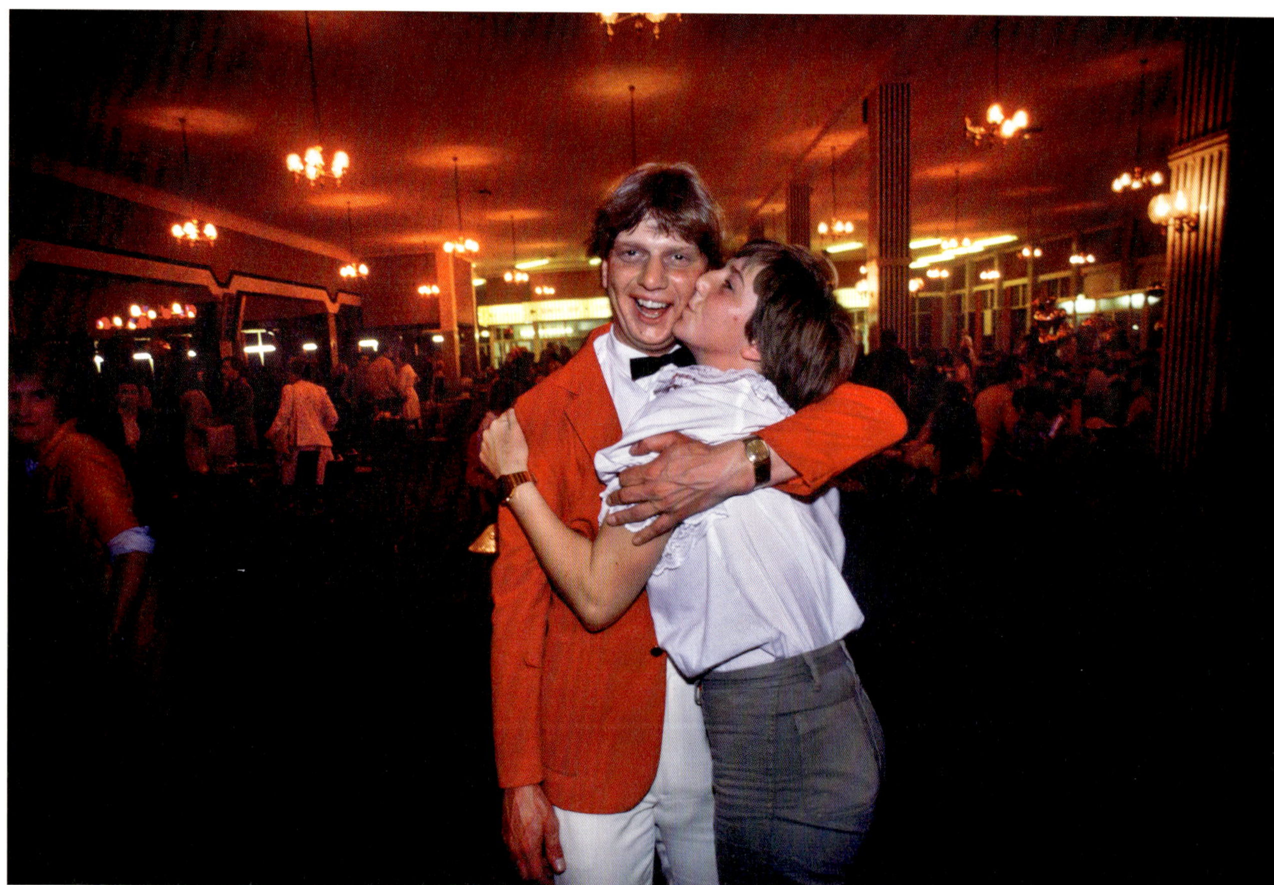

It's time to dance the Butlin's waltz
It's time to say goodnight
It's time for sweet and pleasant dreams
Until the morning light
So go to bed each sleepy head
And as we dream we'll say
Thank you Mr Butlin for a very happy day

Extract from the song 'Butlin's Waltz'

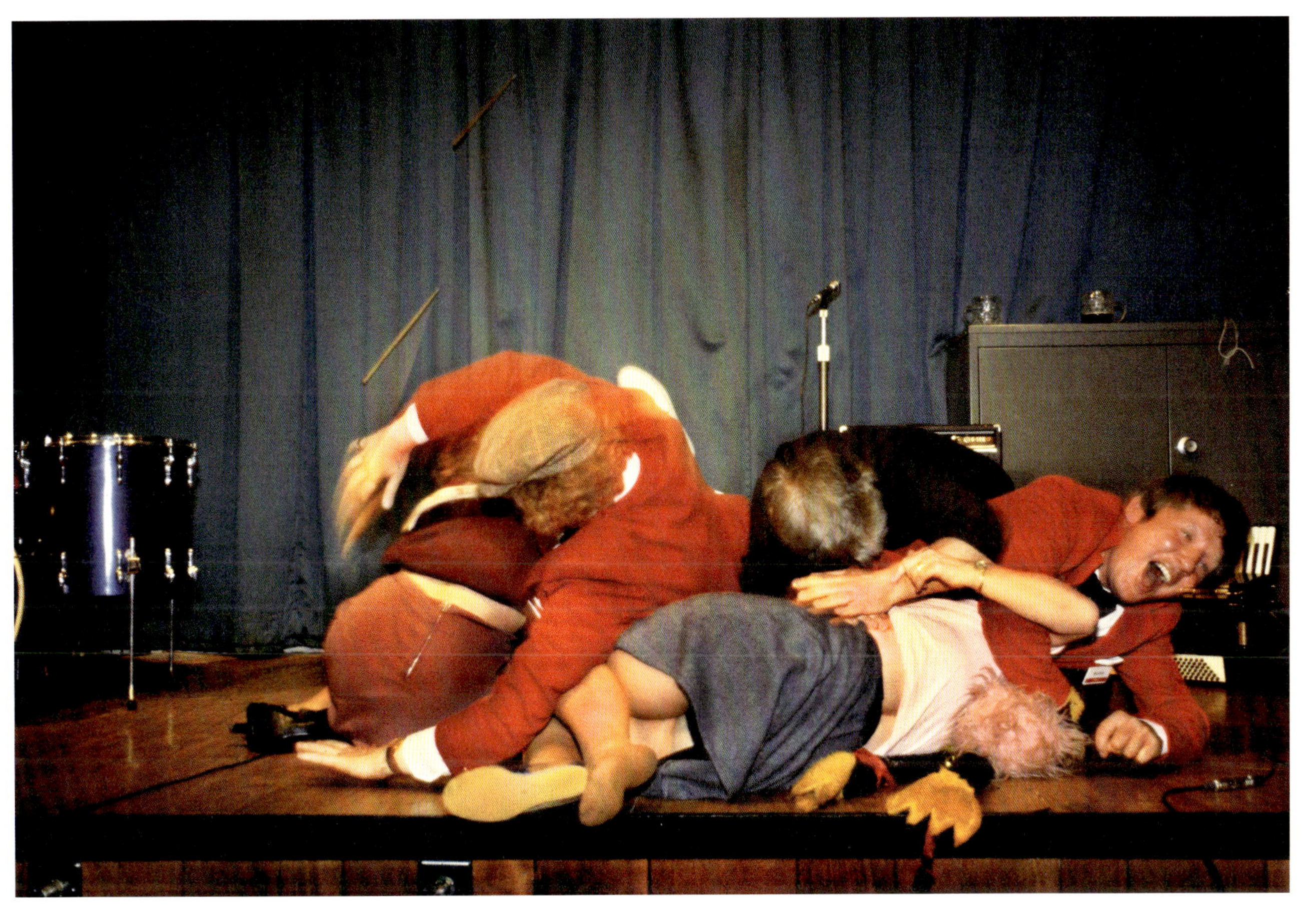

A joint stage performance of Redcoats and campers during an evening show.

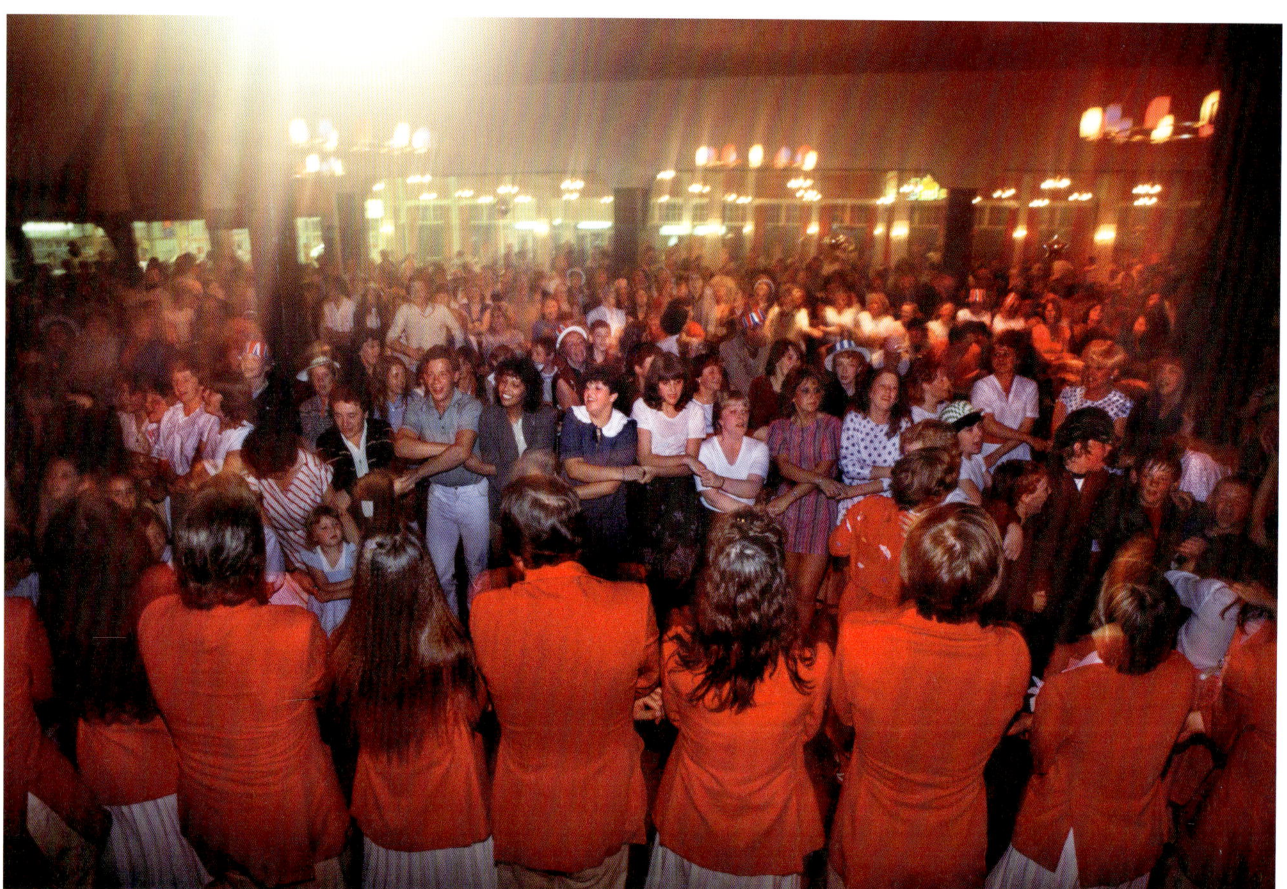

Goodnight campers, I can see you yawning
Goodnight campers, see you in the morning
You must cheer up or you'll soon be dead
For I've heard it said
Folks die in bed

Extract from the song 'Goodnight, Campers'

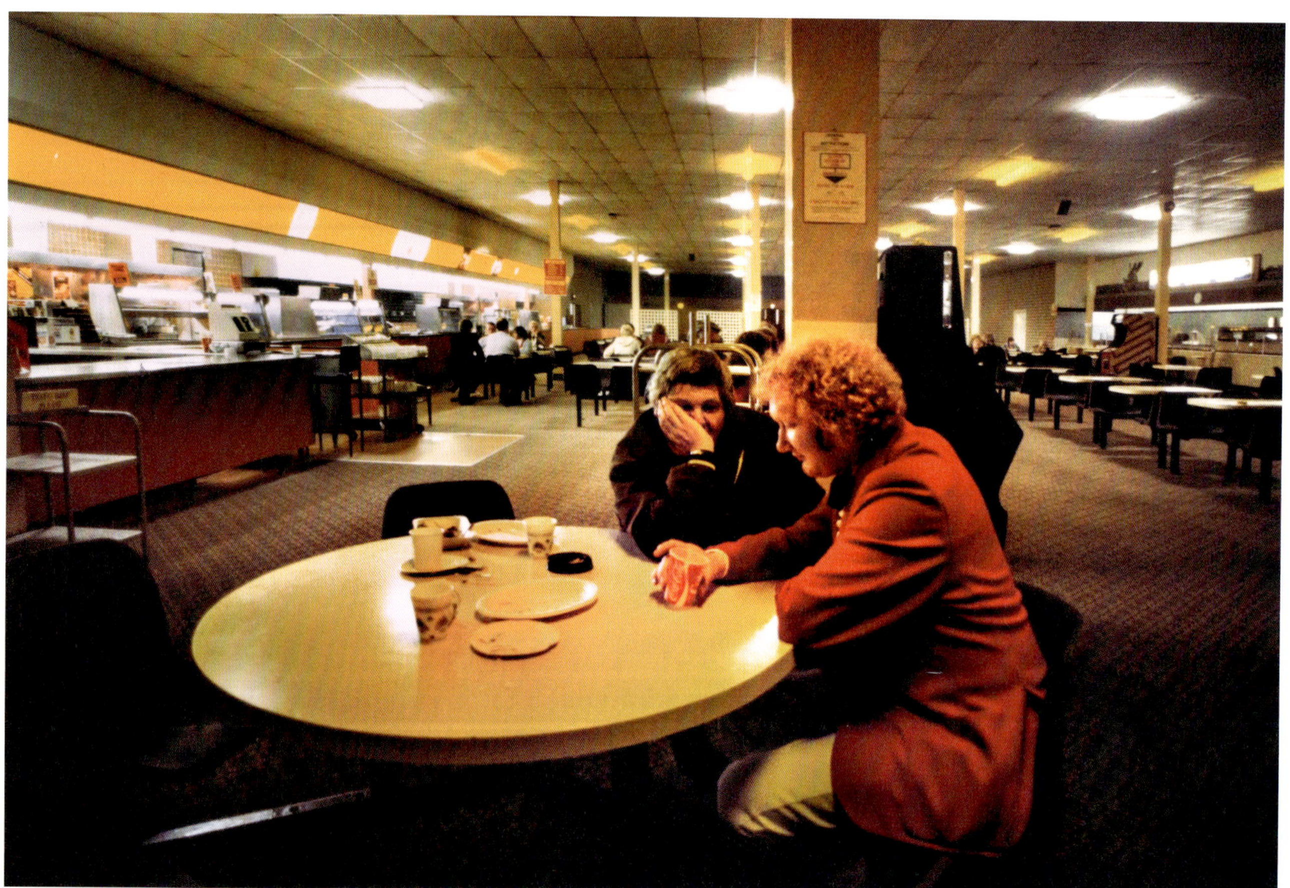

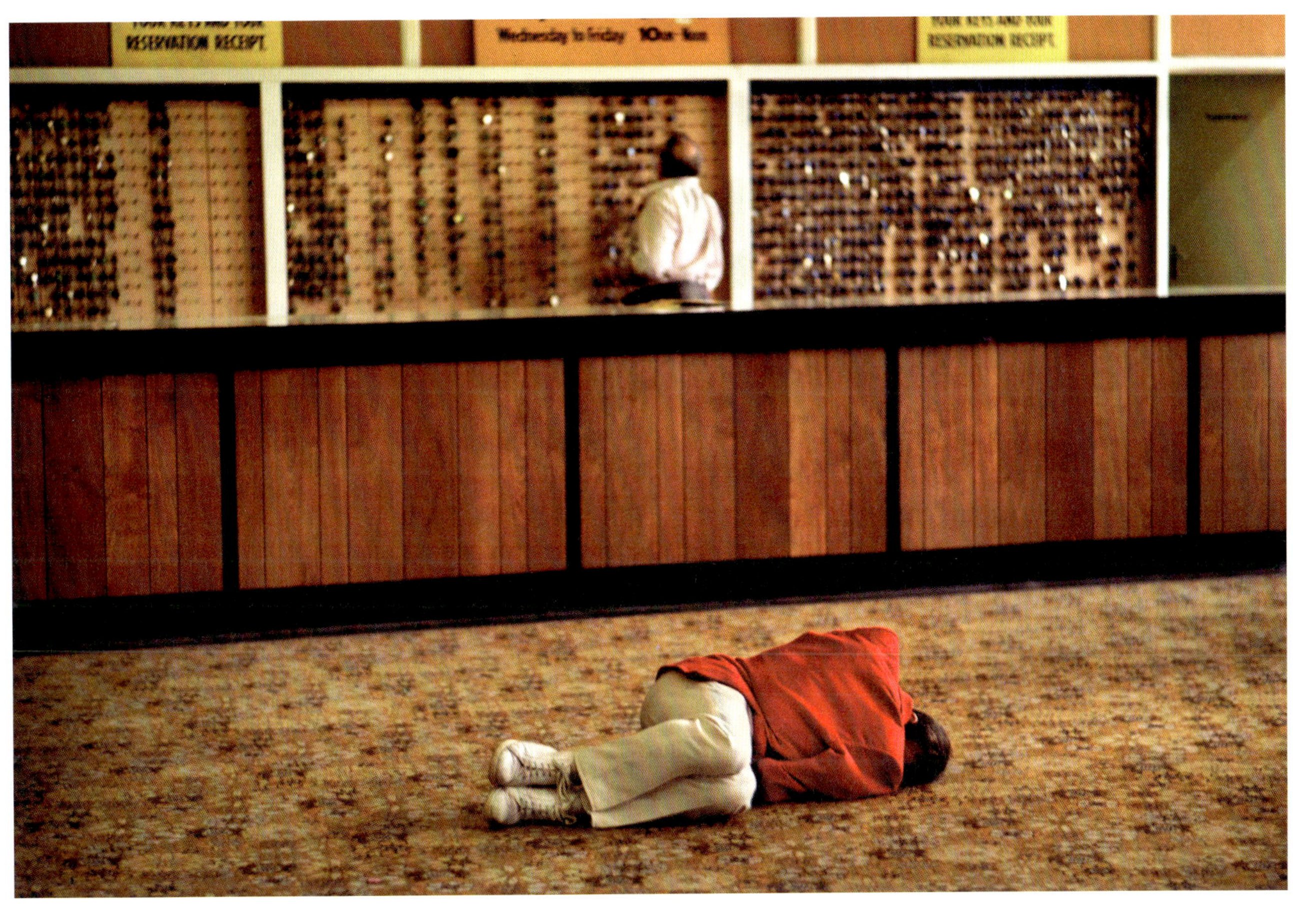

Saturday morning: a Redcoat sits in contemplation during the early hours while another sleeps off the night before in the lobby.

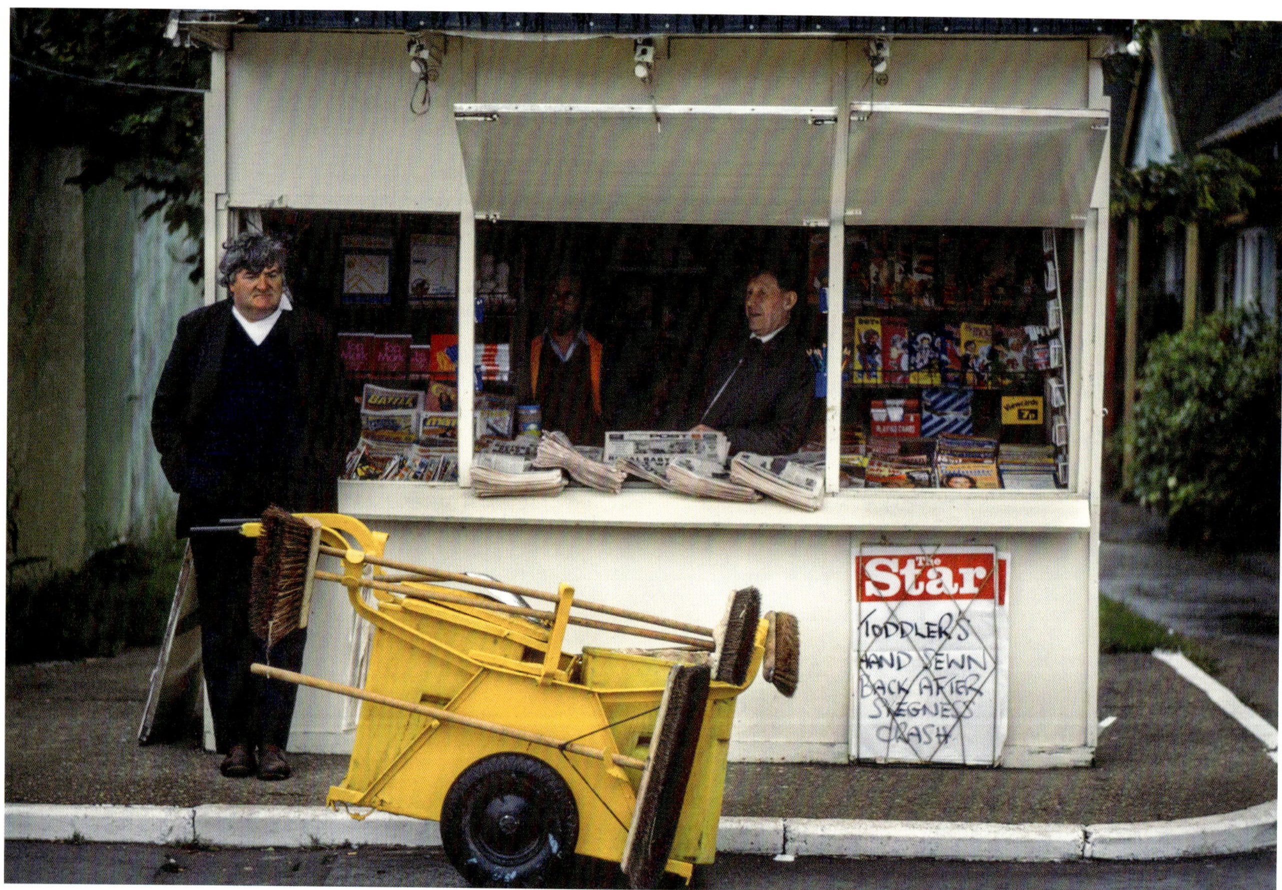
BATTLE
The
Star
TODDLERS
HAND SEWN
BACK AFTER
SKEGNESS
CRASH

**Roll out of bed in the morning
With a great big smile and a good, good morning
Wake up with a grin
There's a new day a-tumbling in**

Extract from the song 'Good Morning, Campers'

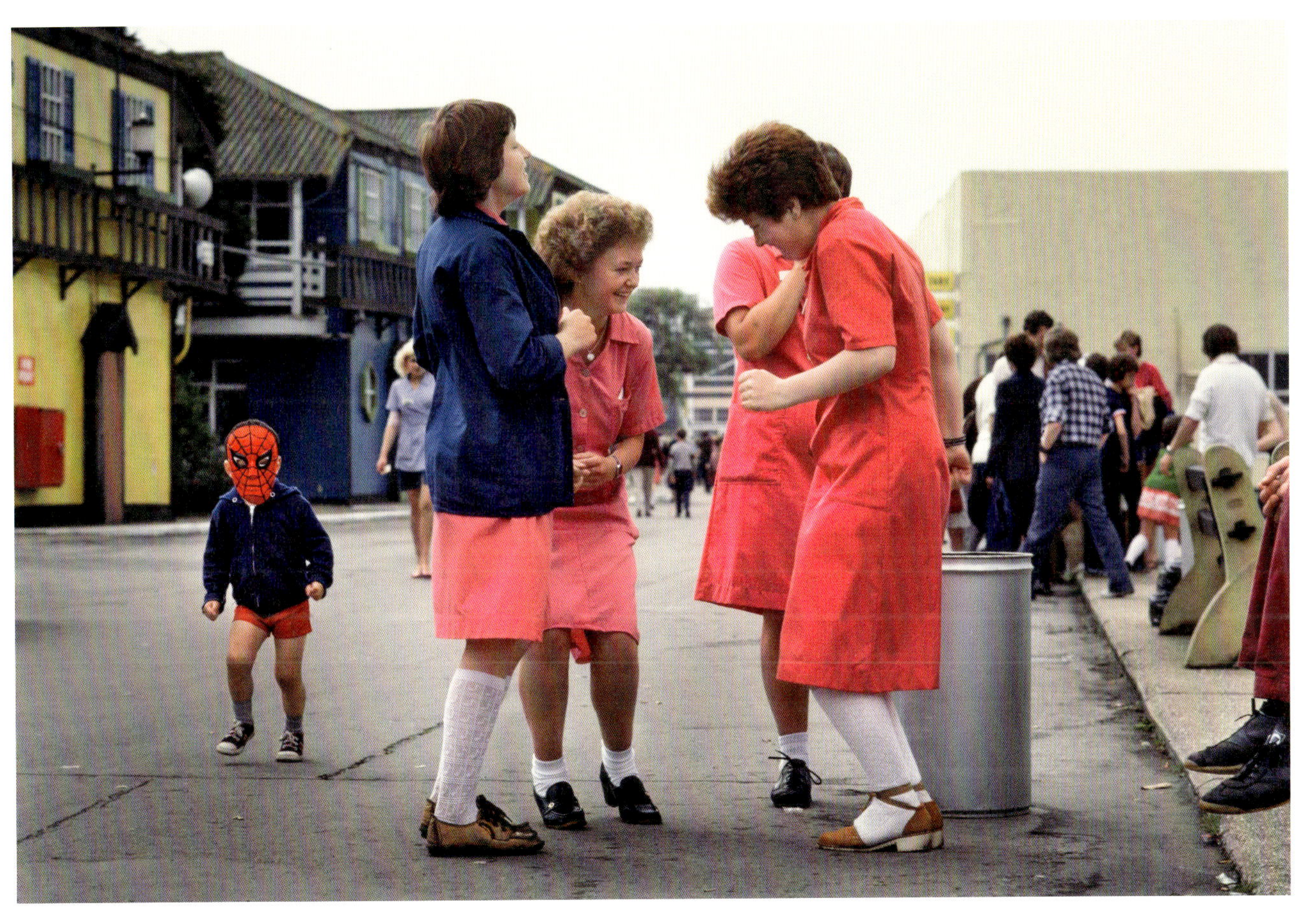

Chambermaids enjoying their break on a Saturday morning.

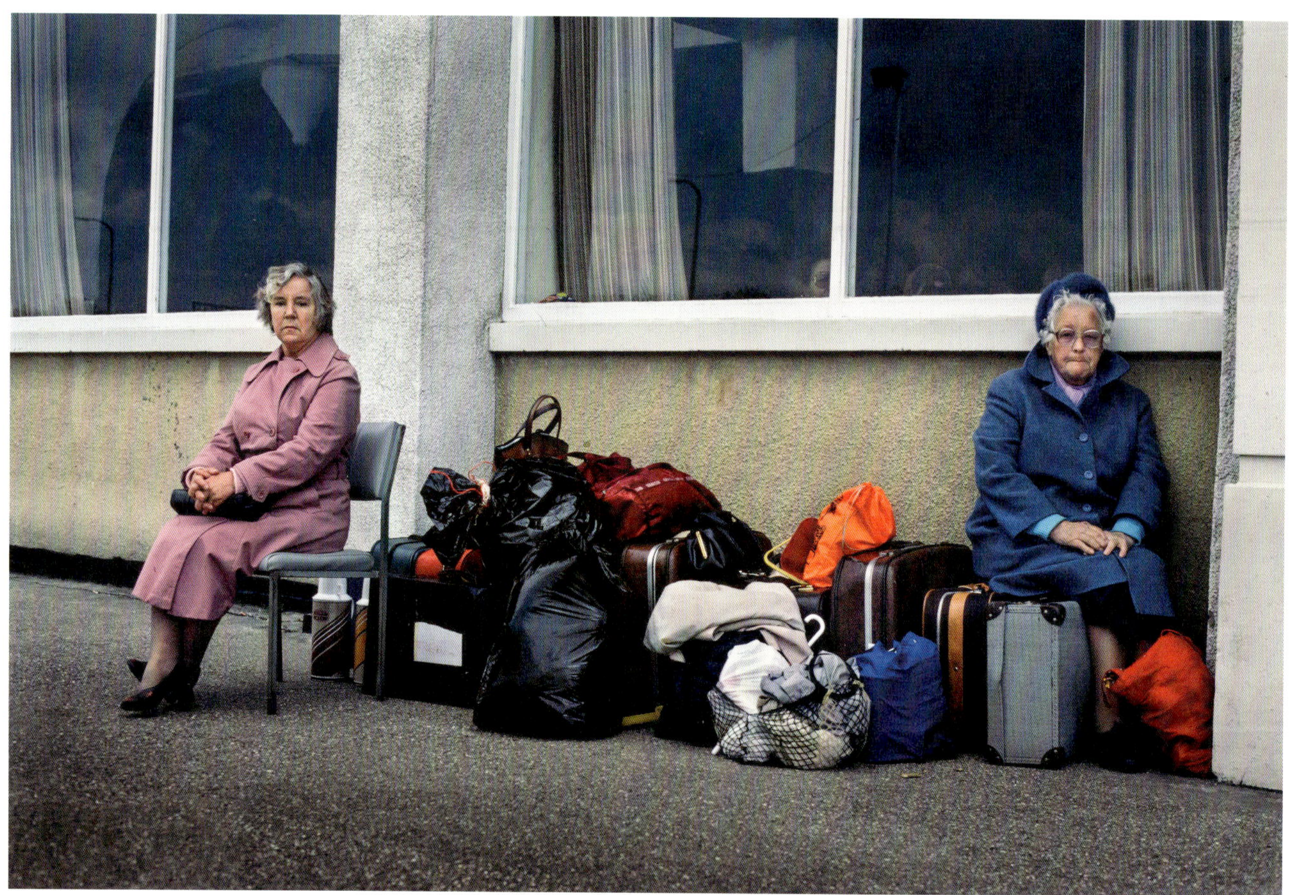

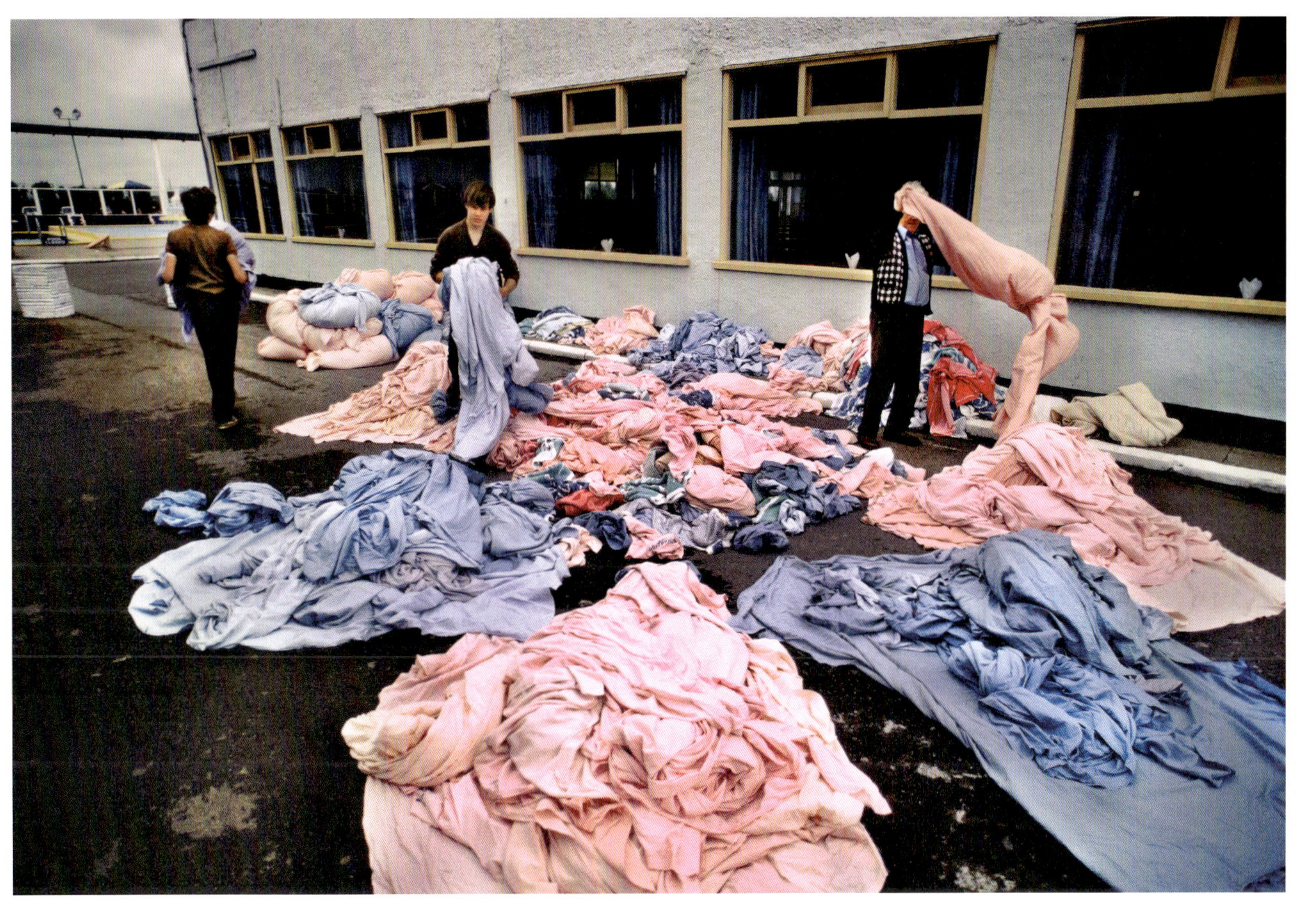

Departing guests, packed up and waiting for the coach home,
while staff sort through the week's laundry.

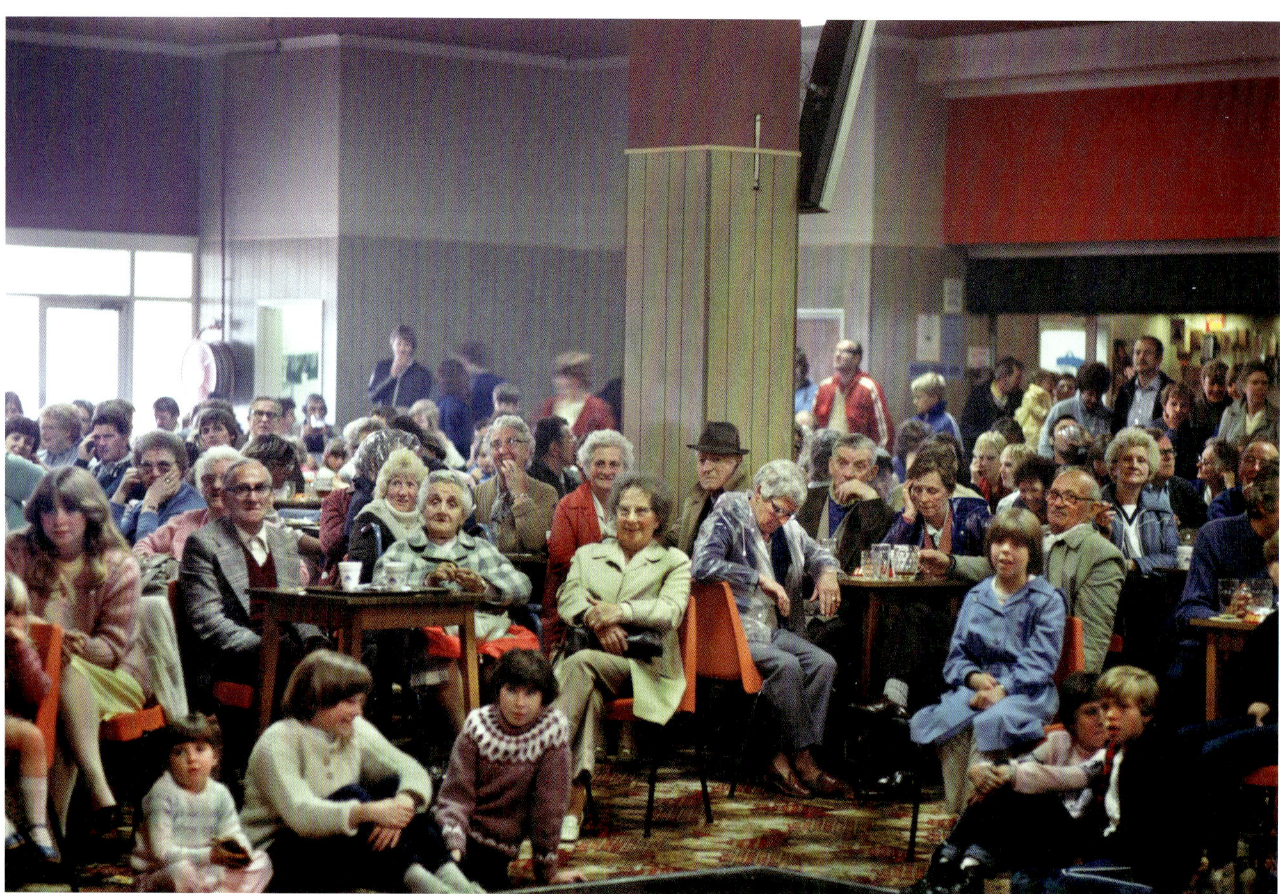

We'll meet again
We all know when
Next holiday at Butlin's
We won't forget
The friends we met
On holiday at Butlin's

Extract from the song 'A Holiday at Butlin's'

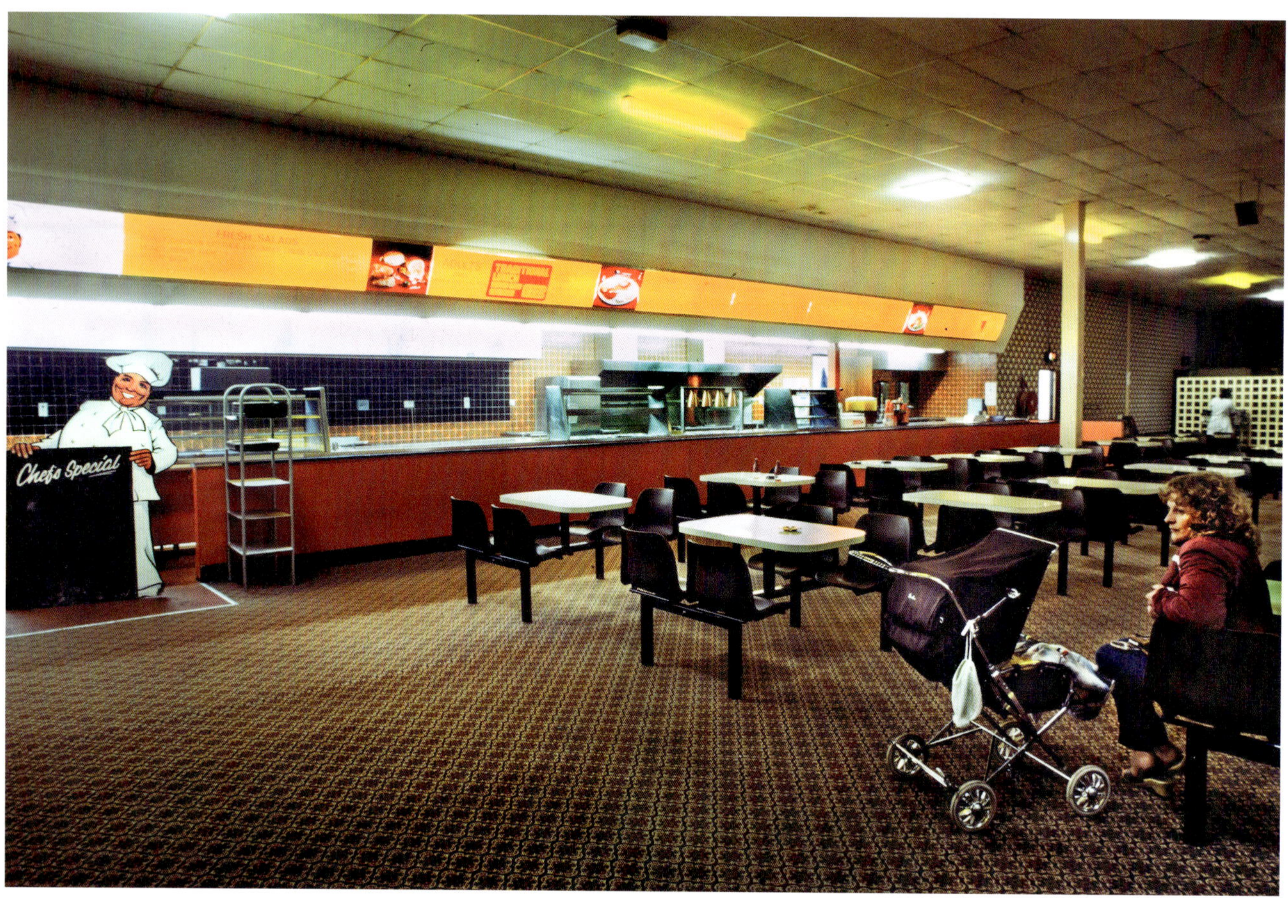

Chef's Special

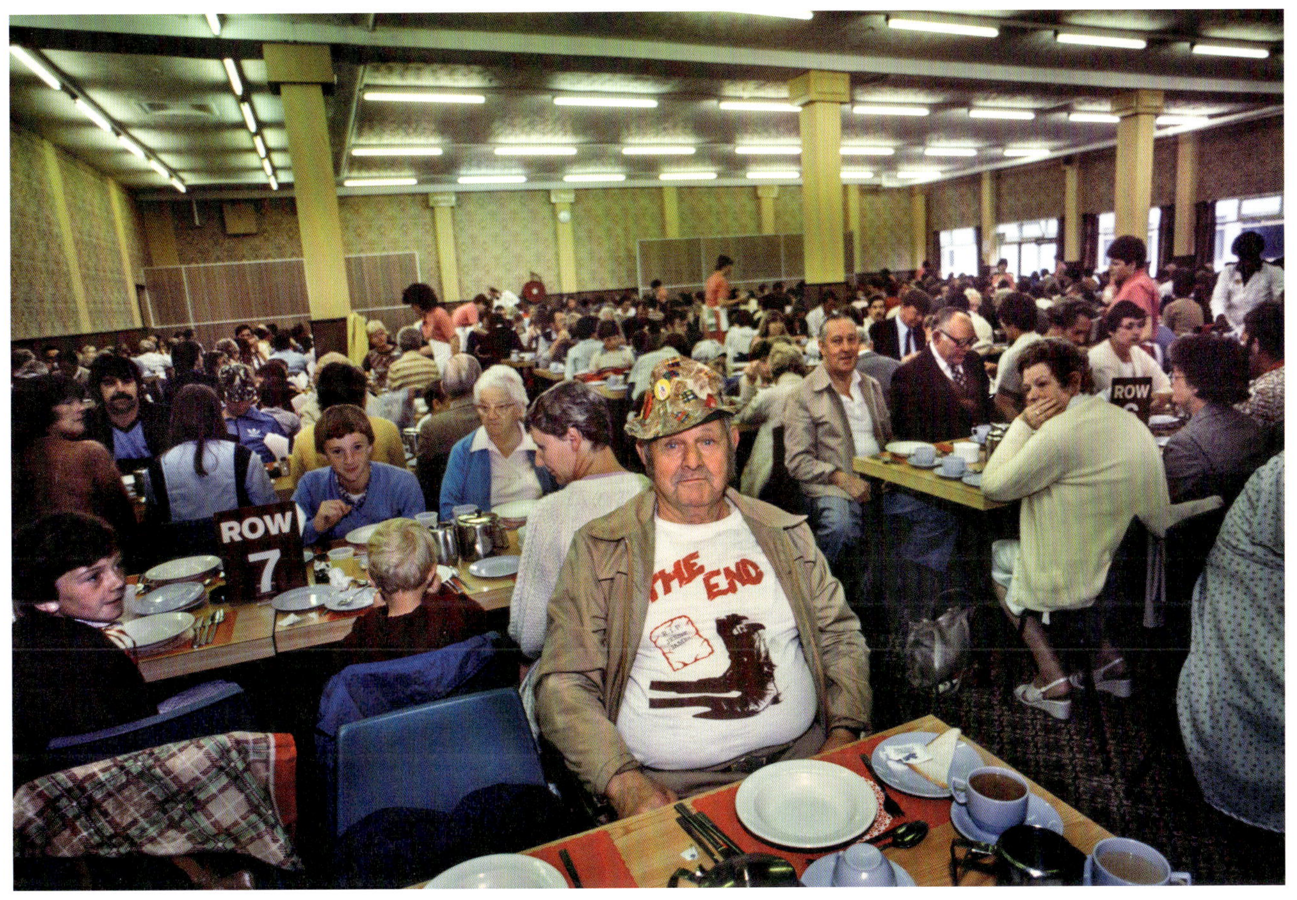

Saturday morning: waiting for the final breakfast in the cafeteria and dining hall.

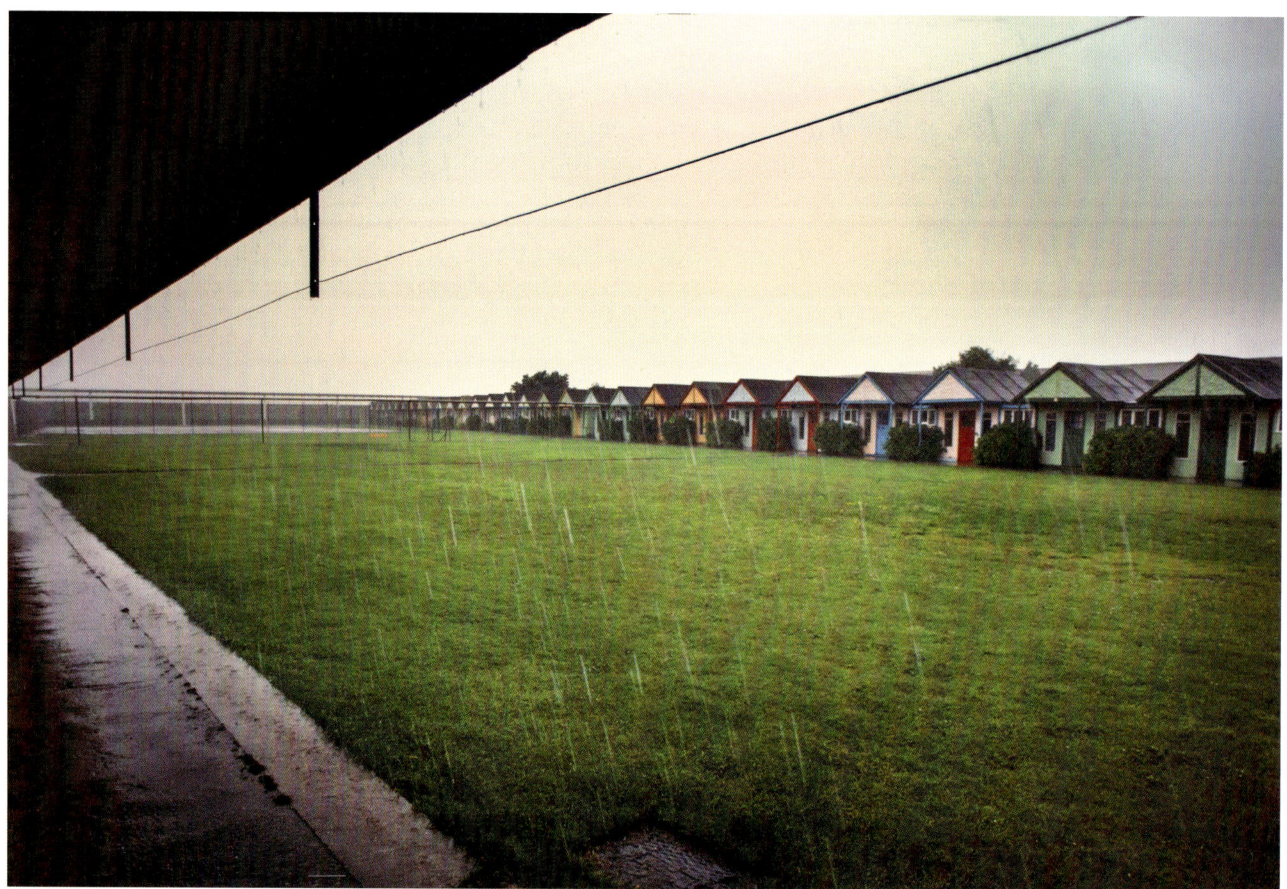

Skegness is so bracing.

Part of the epitaph on Billy Butlin's grave

THANKS

Many thanks to all those who have made this book possible: the photographers and staff at Network who encouraged my work and who shared our vibrant community and practice for over 20 years; Colin Jacobson, a legendary picture editor who, while at the *Observer Magazine,* commissioned my trips to Butlin's; Val Williams and Karen Shepherdson who incorporated some of my photographs from Butlin's into their *Seaside: Photographed* exhibition which opened at Turner Contemporary in Margate and tours Britain in 2020.

For supplying and researching early publicity images, I would like to thank Andrew French at Butlin's and Eve Read. And thanks to Kev for his 'Butlin's Memories', a spirited online collection of Butlin's memorabilia, images and songs. Most importantly, I want to thank all of the Butlin's staff for always looking on the bright side, even when it rained for much of the time!

Thanks to Martin, Ann and all the staff at Hoxton Mini Press who, along with the designer Friederike Huber, made this book happen. Hannah Charlton, my other half, who edits and encourages with endless patience and humour.

Finally, this is a tribute to my friend and colleague, the writer Ian Walker [1952–1990], who worked with me on the original story and, as always, told it how it really was.

Barry Lewis

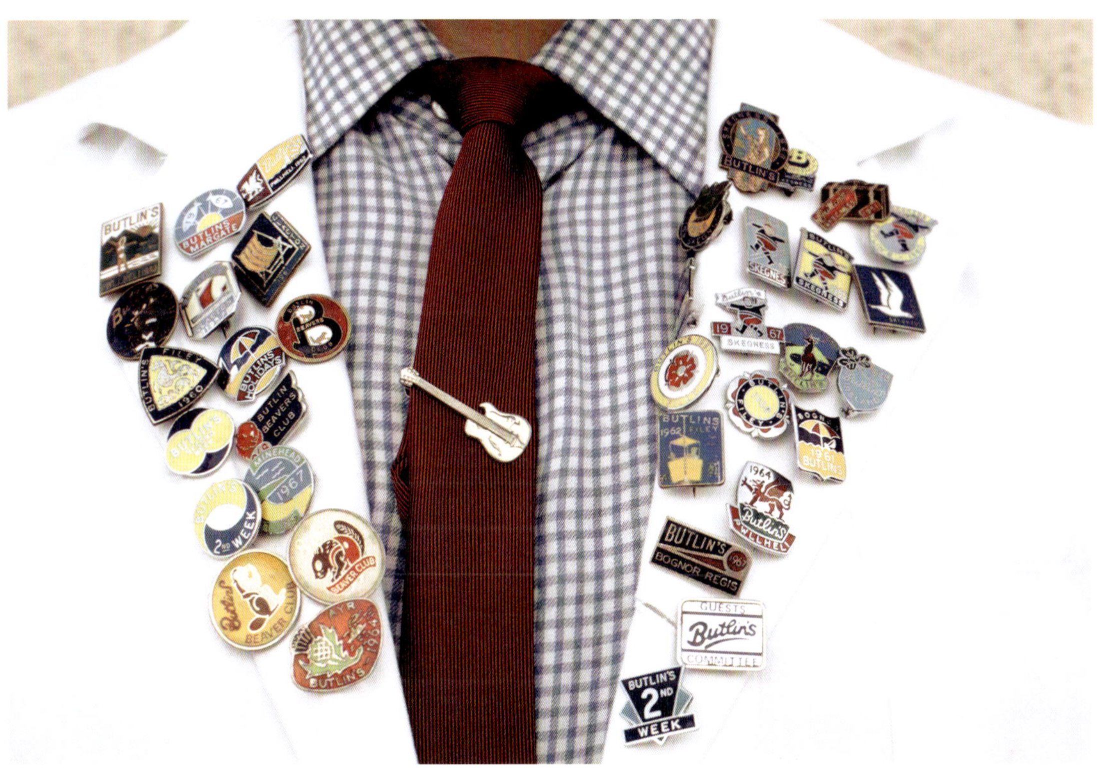

A kitchen manager proudly wearing his vintage collection
of identity badges, used for camp entry until 1967

Butlin's Holiday Camp 1982

First edition, published 2020
by Hoxton Mini Press, London
www.hoxtonminipress.com

ISBN: 978-1-910566-72-5

A CIP catalogue record for this book is available from the British Library.

Printed and bound by Artron, China

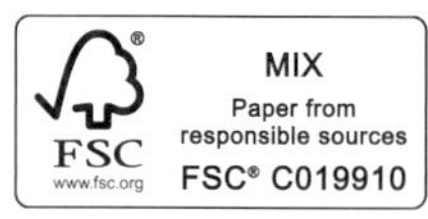